The Rāmāyaṇa Culture
Text, Performance and Iconography

The Rāmāyaṇa Culture

Text, Performance and Iconography

Edited by

Mandakranta Bose

PRINTWORLD

Publishers of Indian Traditions

Cataloging in Publication Data — DK
[Courtesy: D.K. Agencies (P) Ltd. <docinfo@dkagencies.com>]

Conference: the Rāmāyaṇa Culture: Text, Performance, Iconography and Gender (1999 : Vancouver, B.C.)
The Rāmāyaṇa culture : text, performance, and iconography / edited by Mandakranta Bose.
pages cm
"Papers from the Conference: the Rāmāyaṇa Culture: Text, Performance, Iconography and Gender held in the Vancouver, February 19-20, 1999" – Title page verso.
"First published in 2000 under the title: A varied optic: contemporary studies in the Rāmāyaṇa by the Institute of Asian Research, The University of British Columbia, Vancouver, Canada. Second revised edition published in India in 2003" – Title page verso.
Includes bibliographical references and index.
ISBN 9788124602249

1. Vālmīki. Rāmāyaṇa – Congresses. 2. Hindu literature – History and criticism – Congresses. 3. Art, Hindu – Congresses. 4. Hindu symbolism – Congresses. I. Bose, Mandakranta, 1938- editor. II. Varied optic. III. Title.

LCC BL1139.26.V353C66 1999 | DDC 294.5922046 23

Papers from the conference: The *Rāmāyaṇa* Culture: Text, Performance, Iconography and Gender held in the Vancouver, February 19-20, 1999.

First published in 2000 under the title *A Varied Optic: Contemporary Studies in the Rāmāyaṇa* by the Institute of Asian Research, The University of British Columbia, Vancouver, Canada.

Second revised edition published in India in 2003
Reprinted in 2020

ISBN 978-81-246-0224-9

Printed and published by:
D.K. Printworld (P) Ltd.
Regd. office : *Vedaśrī*, F-395, Sudarshan Park
(Metro Station: ESI Hospital)
New Delhi - 110 015
Phones: (011) 2545 3975, 2546 6019
E-mail: indology@dkprintworld.com
Web: www.dkprintworld.com

Acknowledgements

SINCE this book originated in a conference, 'The *Ramayana* Culture: Text, Performance, Iconography and Gender', at the University of British Columbia, the first debt I must acknowledge is to those who made the gathering possible with financial and organisational assistance: the Institute of Asian Research, the Centre for India and South Asia Research, and the Office of the Dean of Graduate Studies. I am grateful to the Centre for India and South Asia Research and the Publications Committee of the Institute of Asian Research for providing funds for the publication of this volume.

My colleagues have helped me in many ways, intellectual and practical; to them, my thanks. I am also grateful to several students who worked with me to make the conference successful. It is a pleasure to acknowledge my gratitude to Robert Faulkner who worked tirelessly on the page-design of the book and prepared a camera-ready copy, Michael Dowad who provided the photograph for the cover, and my daughter Sarika Bose who drew the illustrations. My thanks are due also to Ms. Amandeep Mann for meticulously correcting the typographical errors in the first edition.

I am grateful to Mr. Susheel K. Mittal of D.K. Printworld for bringing out this, the revised second edition, and for taking as much care to ensure both accuracy and elegance in its production as he did for my *Speaking of Dance*.

Mandakranta Bose

Preface
to the Second and Revised Edition

THIS monograph was first published in 2001 as an in-house publication for the Centre for India and South Asia Research at the Institute of Asian Research, University of British Columbia. The task was a daunting one since it had to be completed in time for another conference on the *Rāmāyaṇa* that soon followed. The process of switching between computers that used different fonts with varying diacritical marks made the task even more challenging. With that deadline in view, the volume was printed from a camera-ready copy, which unfortunately resulted in a number of serious typographical errors. Since then, a number of corrections and revisions have been made, including some by the authors, and the present volume, I hope, will do justice both to the subject and to the authors.

Mandakranta Bose

Preface to the First Edition

THE articles that comprise this volume originated in a two-day conference entitled, 'The *Rāmāyaṇa* Culture: Text, Performance, Iconography and Gender', at the Institute of Asian Research, University of British Columbia, on 19 and 20 February 1999. This gathering of *Rāmāyaṇa* scholars from Canada, USA, England and the University of British Columbia was organised by the Programme in Intercultural Studies in Asia at the Institute of Asian Research, with support from the Centre for India and South Asia Research of the Institute. The conference was planned as the first step towards launching an ambitious and long-term project on the enduring presence of the *Rāmāyaṇa* in the varied political and cultural domains of South and South-East Asia. Over almost two millennia the mythic world of Rāma, Sītā, Lakṣmaṇa and Hanumān has proved to be an ethical, political and cultural imaginary from which present-day public life continues to draw artistic as well as pragmatic paradigms. Not confined within the often uncritical prestige enjoyed by a 'classic' literary work, the *Rāmāyaṇa* has been the subject of lively debate, including sharply partisan critiques, especially in recent years. The object of this modest volume is to participate in that debate and perhaps to make some contribution to it.

While the contributors look at the *Rāmāyaṇa* from distinctly different angles, they converge to a central aspiration of current scholarship, namely, understanding the way in which the epic constructs aesthetic and ideological meaning for the modern consciousness. The five essays in the present volume and the introduction span several critical areas. The first essay examines what might be termed the contentious issue of Vālmīki's seminal status and the underlying debate on canonicity itself in present-day *Rāmāyaṇa* scholarship. This is followed by a study of the iconography of the *Rāmāyaṇa* derived from an alternate tradition located in Indonesia. The remaining essays raise and analyse some of the gender issues implicit in the epic, taking into their purview not only what has been commonly taken as the 'central' text but 'peripheral' ones as well. In doing so, these studies venture even beyond the textual level to other forms of cultural representation.

This volume makes no claim of establishing a bridgehead; there has never been a lack of scholarly interest in the *Rāmāyaṇa*. Much has been written and many conferences held in India, in other South and South-East Asian countries and in the West. Modern editions have appeared based on imaginative and sophisticated textual research, the work on the *Vālmīki Rāmāyaṇa* by Robert Goldman and Sally Sutherland Goldman being a major exemplar. John Brockington's studies in the *Rāmāyaṇa* and the *Mahābhārata* have contributed much to our knowledge. A specially exciting field has opened up with the study of regional versions of the *Rāmāyaṇa* popular in different parts of India, and this trend of admitting popular traditions into the research domain of the 'classics' has led to the recognition of such alternate renderings of the epic as those by women. Studies abound both in popular as well as in Sanskrit *Rāmāyaṇas*. In view of the new light thrown on the epic by a host of scholars — Paula Richman, Philip Lutgendorf, Sally Sutherland-Goldman, Robert Goldman, Monika Boehm-Tettelbach (a.k.a. Thiel-Horstmann), William Smith, Narayan Rao, to name only a few — one may well wonder what need there might be for yet another book such as this. But as noted above, we have indeed entered a particularly fruitful era of enquiry in which many of the *donnée* of a canonical critique have come under informed interrogation. It is hoped that the present volume will justify itself by demonstrating the vigour of that interrogation.

The book falls into a two-part structure, the first comprising two essays, by Robert Goldman and Alessandra Lopez y Royo, which might be thought of as a debate on 'classicness' or, to use different terms, centre and periphery. Robert Goldman's essay situates this volume in a much larger discussion, namely, the effort in recent scholarship about India on making subaltern, neglected, and marginal voices central. Reviewing recent the trend in *Rāmāyaṇa* scholarship to resist the privileging of Vālmīki as the pointman of patriarchy, Goldman makes a spirited textual case for recognising him as the *ādikavi*, the First Poet, whose text has resonated with the changing ethical, aesthetic and political sensibilities of succeeding ages, encompassing and empowering multiple subject positions. As he makes plain, this is also a discussion that has a specific profile in recent studies and discussions concerning the *Rāmāyaṇa* itself.

Alessandra Lopez y Royo's essay, which follows Goldman's, goes some way toward suggesting that the aversion to Vālmīki's hegemony is actually not without its own logic. Her argument develops along two lines. First, Dr. y Royo works in a medium quite different from the textual, a medium that establishes its own meanings of what constitutes canon: that is, art/sculpture. Second, she rightly objects to the fact that there is an enduring tendency to regard South-East Asian versions of the *Rāmāyaṇa* as derivative of Indian ones, relegating them to second-best status. Given the prestige of the epic in South-East Asia and its close involvement with the business of rulership, she is surely right to reject this Indianist bias. Hence her piece is featured in the volume as an attempt to recognise an alternate classic. This does not undermine the case Goldman makes, but it does show what the debate is about.

Placing the debate in the arena of gender issues, the three other essays form a natural group, addressing as they do the variously realised position of women in the epic. The gender issue has, in fact, been a major way in which 'classicness' has been contested — and so represented in recent scholarship. Heidi Pauwels' chapter on three iterations of the *phulvārī* episode looks into the idealisation of love and its formulation as arranged marriage. Pauwels not only explicates the theme within its textual boundary but moves it farther to a different domain of cultural production, namely, Bombay cinema, and more particularly, the vastly influential TV *Rāmāyaṇa* by Ramanand Sagar.

Vidyut Aklujkar's essay on Kaikeyī in the *Ānanda Rāmāyaṇa* introduces a text that is little known but was surprisingly influential in its period, and takes us to a figure who is critical to the development of the epic, in whatever form. Marking the contrast to Sītā, who is Pauwels' focus, and the fact that Kaikeyī has in the *AR* a shadow woman behind her — the querulous Kalahā from a former life — Aklujkar helps to deepen our picture of the sorts of levels the epic as a whole can plumb. Thereby this essay shows how much is lost of the culture engendered by the epic if one remains chained to Vālmīki and ignores the alternate tradition of the *Rāmāyaṇa*.

The last essay is Sally Sutherland Goldman's interpretation of the role of ornament in Vālmīki's epic as a sign of sexual activity. Providing a symmetrical *finale* to the collection, this essay brings us back to Vālmīki, but in the 'female' mode.

Having moved quite some way through the two preceding chapters into the terrain of issues focusing on women by the time we arrive here, we have a clear sense of how Vālmīki is able to take a subset of gender issues and make them truly work as a classic.

It is hoped that the book will produce considerable interest, admittedly within an academic frame, which is stimulated by the fact that there have been three other notable collections of essays on the *Rāmāyaṇa* in recent years that establish a lineage for this volume, two edited by Paula Richman (one of them forthcoming) and the other by Monika Boehm-Tettelbach (a.k.a. Thiel-Horstmann). It is hoped that the present collection will be found to enhance the ongoing discussion as the latest instalment, something that marks the current state of the debate.

Mandakranta Bose

Contents

Introduction

WHY has the *Rāmāyaṇa* been so popular for so long a time in India and in many parts of South and South-East Asia? What does it offer to the millions who have been enthralled through the centuries by the stories of its heroes, demons, magical beasts and birds, the moral questions they raise to highlight as many dilemmas as prescriptions? Is it the primal appeal of the victory of good over evil? Is it the didactic projection of Rāma and Sītā as role models for common mortals, both male and female, Rāma being the ideal son, husband, brother, the perfect king, dutiful and selfless, and Sītā, the ideal of wifely devotion? Or, is it the allegory of devotion and total surrender, *bhakti* and *prapatti*, one sees in the story of Rāma, the Godhead whose grace brings order into chaos and lays an inalienable claim upon the human soul as represented by Sītā? For many people, of course, the *Rāmāyaṇa* is mainly entertainment. The arts traditions of India, Thailand, Kampuchea and Indonesia, including literature, painting, sculpture and the performing arts, have drawn upon the *Rāmāyaṇa* widely and creatively. Its public profile in India was enhanced dramatically in the 1980s with its serialisation in a television version of such popularity that during its weekly screenings business came to a virtual halt all over India and acquired an enthusiastic following among people of South and South-East Asian origin living abroad. In recent times, the epic has entered the political arena as well. Beginning with Gandhi's vision of *Rāmrājya* in the twentieth century and influencing the current Rām-

Janambhūmi debate in India, the ideals of the *Rāmāyaṇa* have continued to claim public attention if not invariable allegiance.

Clearly, the *Rāmāyaṇa* means many things to many people. From this one may infer that even though there is one dominant text of the epic, there are in fact many *Rāmāyaṇas*, to use Paula Richman's phrase,[1] which must be studied and perhaps simultaneously deconstructed and remembered in order to understand what the epic means and how. But although scholarship has never neglected the *Rāmāyaṇa*, it was only in the later half of the twentieth century that scholarship began to take this varied approach, as noted in the Preface. Few things better attest to the disciplined reconsideration of India in all of the signification that one may attach to the term 'India', than the questioning to which scholarship is now subjecting the *Rāmāyaṇa*, a commanding icon of Indianness if ever there was one.

Recent research initiatives span a wide terrain. In textual studies we are beginning to enjoy the products of editorial efforts grounded in scientific studies in textual variants and transmission,[2] as well as of literary analyses that apply formalist, semantic and deconstructionist methods. Not only in methodology but in coverage of new ground one finds sustained expansion, as for instance, the sociology and politics of the epic and the performance arts nurtured by it. Particular vigour has been gained in all of these fields through subaltern and feminist analyses.

Yet, far from exhausting research possibilities in the

1. Paula Richman, ed., *Many Rāmāyaṇas: The Diversity of a Narrative Tradition in South Asia* (Berkeley and Los Angeles: University of California Press, 1992).
2. Including computer analyses of the text, such as Kenneth Bryant's work in progress.

Rāmāyaṇa, scholarship has left many areas still unexplored, especially in regional traditions of both text and performance. Cross-disciplinary or cross-genre critiques are few and brief, and even though most areas of information were mapped by the beginning of the twentieth century, sustained treatments of particular aspects of the epic are often lacking. To take only one of many examples, I may cite the meagre attention paid to one of the most influential of regional *Rāmāyaṇas*, the version by Kṛttibāsa, a fourteenth-century Bengālī poet. Admittedly, histories of Bengālī literature, notably that by Dinesh Chandra Sen, and the meticulous study of eastern traditions of the *Rāmāyaṇa* by William Smith, the latter in particular, provide vital information about the author and set his work in the larger framework of the social history and poetic practices of eastern India.[3] But Kṛttibāsa's original rendition of Vālmīki's poem has been overlaid by so many interpolations through the six centuries after him that what passes now as his *Rāmāyaṇa* is not so much his work — and even less of Vālmīki's — as a tapestry of the collective consciousness of the Bengālī speaking peoples of eastern India that records their changing beliefs and practices.

The need for studying that complex representation in closer detail than attempted so far was dramatically demonstrated to me sometime ago when I came upon the story of Bhagīratha, the king who brought the river goddess Gaṅgā to the earth from her heavenly abode. Part of the genealogical history of Rāma, this episode had escaped my attention, nor had it been narrated to me by any of my elders in my childhood — for reasons not hard to comprehend.

3. Dinesh Chandra Sen, *History of Bengali Language and Literature* (Calcutta: University of Calcutta, 1954); William Smith, *Rāmāyaṇa Traditions in Eastern India* (Stockholm: University of Stockholm, 1988).

As a Bengālī child I knew the name Kṛttibāsa from early days but grew up with the abridged version of the *Kṛttibāsī Rāmāyaṇa* (as it is known in Bengal) for children by Upendra Kishore Roy Choudhury which carefully excises the Uttara Kāṇḍa.[4] So the story I read had a happy ending with everybody living happily together after Rāma, Sītā and Lakṣmaṇa return to Ayodhyā. Later, as a small child, I remember watching a film called *Rāmarājya*, which showed Sītā being swallowed by the earth. I was upset although very happy to learn that the earth was Sītā's mother and that Sītā had found refuge in her mother's lap. But this made me wonder whether there was more to the *Rāmāyaṇa* beyond the story I had read. Through the years I discovered that there were indeed many strange episodes in the *Rāmāyaṇa* not only of Kṛttibāsa but those of Tulasī Dās and even of Vālmīki himself. But none compares in oddness with the Bhagīratha story in Ādi Kāṇḍa of the *Kṛttibāsī Rāmāyaṇa*.

The story begins with King Sagara who loses his sixty thousand sons to the wrath of Kapilamuni whose angry gaze burns them to cinders, which prevents them from receiving proper funerary rites. The sage tells Aṅśumān, Sagara's grandson, that the sons of Sagara would find release if one of their descendants could bring Gaṅgā from heaven to wash over the ashes. Beginning with Sagara himself, every king in each generation of that dynasty undertakes many austerities and penances but fails to bring the Gaṅgā to earth. The crisis deepens when Dilīp, the great-grandson of Sagara, dies without leaving any child to carry on the quest. The crisis is resolved thus:

mariyā dilīp rājā gela brahmaloka ॥

4. Upendrakishore Roy Choudhury, *Cheleder Rāmāyaṇa* (Calcutta: Nirmal Book Agency, 1995).

arājak haila rājya ayodhyā-nagara ।
svargete cintita brahmā āra purandara ॥

śuniyāchi janmibena viṣṇu sūryakūle ।
kemane bāḍibe vaṁṣa nirmūla haile ॥

bhāviyā sakala deva yukti kari mane ।
ayodhyay pāṭhāila prabhu trilocane ॥

dilipera dui jāyā āchilena bāse ।
vṛṣa ārohaṇe śiva gelena sakāśe ॥

kahilena doṁhākāra prati tripurāri ।
mama vare putravatī habe eka nārī ॥

dui nārī kahe, śuni śivera vacana ।
vidhavā āmarā kise haibe nandana ॥

śaṅkara balen, duijane kara rati ।
mama vare ekera haibe susantati ॥

ei vara diyā gela deva tripurāri ।
snāna kari gela dui dilipera nārī ॥

saṁprītite āchilena se dui yuvatī ।
katadine ekjana haila ṛtumatī ॥

doṁhete jānila yadi doṁhāra sandarbha ।
doṁhe keli karite ekera haila garbha ॥

daśamāsa haila garbha prasava samaya ।
putra peye haraṣita doṁhe gela ghara ॥

āsiyā sakala muni karila kalyāṇa ।
bhage bhage janma hetu bhagīratha nāma ॥

mahākavi kṛttibāsa paṇḍita parama ।
ādikāṇḍe gāna bhagīrathera janama ॥

— *KR*, Ādi Kāṇḍa, pp. 28-29[5]

5. The edition used here is the *Saptakāṇḍa Rāmāyaṇa* (Calcutta: Akshay Library, baṅgābda 1361 [1954]).

> King Dilīp went to *brahmaloka* when he died and the kingdom Ayodhyā became lawless. In heaven, Brahmā and Purandara became worried. [They said,] 'We have heard that Viṣṇu will take birth in the Sūrya dynasty [but] how can that happen if the *vaṁśa* [the line] is extinguished' [lit: rootless]. Having thought [about this], the gods decided to send lord Trilocana [Śiva] to Ayodhyā. The two wives of Dilīp were residing [there and] Śiva went there riding on his bull. Tripurāri told the two women, 'Through my boon one [of you] [lit: woman] will have a son.' Hearing these words of Śiva, the two women said, 'We are widows, how can we have a son?' Śaṅkara said, 'You two copulate and one of you will have a fine son by my boon.' Having bestowed this boon Lord Tripurāri left. The two women took their baths.[6] These two young women enjoyed a close friendship and when one of them entered the menstrual cycle they understood their situation and upon uniting sexually with one another, one conceived. The time of birth approached after the tenth month. . . . Happy at getting a child, the two went home and all the sages came to bless them. Since the son was born from two *bhaga*s [female organs] the [son] was named Bhagīratha. The great poet Kṛttibāsa, a great scholar, [thus] sings at the beginning the [story] of Bhagīratha's birth.

That this bizarre account defies common sense is to put the problem mildly. The biological absurdity apart, what may one infer about social attitudes about sexuality? Does the matter-

6. 'Taking a bath' is an idiomatic expression in Bengālī that signifies the fourth day of a woman's menstrual cycle when she takes a ritual bath and is then ready to conceive.

of-fact reporting of a same-sex relationship indicate that it was common and sanctioned in contemporary society? Or does the context of marvellous happenings suggest that actions, no matter how extraordinary, are validated if ordained by the gods? The textual problem is no less puzzling. I have found no source for the story, which does not occur in Vālmīki's text, nor in Tulasī's. The requirements of the narrative cannot explain the invention either. Producing an offspring is usually not a problem for the story; there are always convenient gods or holy sages to donate their seed, magic potions to ensure conception, and even rape (as in the birth of Bhagīratha's ancestor Hārīta). With these precedents already set, the text had no need to opt for exclusively female progenitors. The account seems decisively feminised. The two women are said to be in a loving relationship, and the narrator goes out of his way to derive the name Bhagīratha from the word *bhaga* (vulva), a forced construction not warranted by Sanskrit usage. Monier-Williams suggests that it is likely derived from *bhagin+ratha* ('having a glorious chariot').[7]

Unexpected turns in a plot, especially additions in a derived narrative, usually signal some special interest on the author's part. What interest might have prompted Kṛttibāsa to invent the Bhagīratha story has escaped me so far but the invention is singular enough to compel investigation on several fronts. The gender element, for instance, is deeper than the unconventional sexuality would suggest; the story goes on to state that the child was born a lump of flesh without bones and was transformed into a properly constituted male child, handsome and strong, only by a boon given by the sage Aṣṭāvakra. Clearly, women may produce offspring on their own without male intervention but not perfect ones. The

7. M. Monier-Williams, *A Sanskrit-English Dictionary* (new edn., Oxford: Clarendon Press, 1960).

biological assumption here is not far from the Aristotelian thesis that women are unrealised men.

The connection between birth and social status also demands attention. Still harping on Bhagīratha's birth, Kṛttibāsa says that at the age of five the child was taunted as a bastard by another boy. But Bhagīratha's mother reassured him by divulging the truth about his divinely ordained birth and his high destiny, that of redeeming his forefathers by bringing Gaṅgā to earth. So predestined, Bhagīratha accomplishes his task and lives on in public memory as a model of resolute virtue. In thus setting aside an origin that would be evidently considered ignominous in the narrator's own society, Kṛittibāsa is surely asserting the superiority of action over birth. A parallel occurs earlier in the same part of Kṛttibāsa's *Rāmāyaṇa*, where the great sage Śukra's daughter Abjā is violently raped by his pupil, King Daṇḍa of the Sūrya dynasty. The sage's wrathful gaze burns the king into ashes and the dynasty is threatened with extinction but is saved when Abjā's illegitimate son Hārīta is acknowledged as the rightful heir to the throne. Taken together, these stories pragmatically place continuity over purity where the survival of lineage is concerned.

The Bhagīratha story also raises the question of reception. How might its sensational lesbianism have been received by Kṛttibāsa's readers? Would they have been offended by this seeming valorization of a sexuality that had no public sanction as far as we know? If they were not, what would be the grounds for exemption? The explanation frequently offered of the marvellous and the supernatural is that they are symbolic expressions of some deep truth. The readiness to discover symbols, however, characterises an academic rather than a mass audience. A likelier explanation, assuming that no reader would take the story as literal truth — the biology is too *outré* for even the most credulous — is that perhaps readers accepted it simply as an artefact having no reference to experiential reality. They would take it as a tale of divine beings and superhuman heroes, and that too in an unimaginably distant past, the truth value of which was so completely unverifiable as to be irrelevant.

But if the story was treated as fantasy, the process and degree of moral instruction the *Rāmāyaṇa* is said to have provided countless generations must be problematic. A narrative that appears as a fantasy and yet provides persuasive guidelines for living must contain quite extraordinarily potent beacons to the moral exemplar, particularly as they are set in so long and complex a narrative. Discovering these cognitive aids and their function is a task that no student of the *Rāmāyaṇa* can afford to neglect.

The problems I have located here in just one episode from only one of the many *Rāmāyaṇas* in existence underscore how much remains to be done in *Rāmāyaṇa* scholarship in general and how many different analytical approaches the task demands. The essays in this collection represent both an awareness of that task and a readiness to venture forth in new directions.

1

The Ghost from the Anthill
Valmīki and the Destiny of the Rāmakathā in South and South-East Asia

R.P. Goldman

Abstract

In this paper I will attempt to draw out several themes in Vālmīki's epic that have kept the legend of Rāma vibrantly alive in the imaginations of the culturally, religiously and linguistically diverse peoples of South and South-East Asia, quite apart from the critical religio-political significance of Rāma in post-twelfth century South Asia. I will also attempt to show why, in an era in which much contemporary *Rāmāyaṇa* scholarship has become so wary of 'privileging' Vālmīki and so focused on versions of the story that allegedly represent anti-Brāhmaṇical or anti-patriarchal constituencies, a thorough knowledge of the 'Ādikāvya' remains central to the field of *Rāmāyaṇa* studies.

I pay homage to the koil, Vālmīki who, having ascended the tree of poetry, perches there sweetly warbling the sweet song, 'Rāma, Rāma!'

For who, having once heard the tale of Rāma, the roar of Vālmīki, lion among sages, who ranges the

> woodlands of poetry, would not attain the highest bliss?
>
> So I pay homage to that blameless sage Prācetasa, who drinks incessantly from the ocean of the nectar of the tale of Rāma, and yet is never sated.[1]

The past dozen years or so have witnessed something of a revival within the Western Indological community of scholarly interest in the study of the *Rāmāyaṇa* in many of the diverse forms in which its has enriched the arts, letters, folk-cultures and devotional traditions of South and South-East Asia for millennia.

Evidence for this can be found in such recent publications as: our ongoing translation of the critical edition of the *Vālmīki Rāmāyaṇa*, Hart and Heifetz's translation of the *Araṇyakāṇḍa* of Kampan's *Irāmāvatāram*, monographs like Lutgendorf's *The Life of a Text: Performing the Rāmcaritmānas* of Tulsī Dās, van der Veer's *Gods on Earth*, Smith's *Rāmāyaṇa Traditions in Eastern India*, Brockington's *Righteous Rāma*, and edited volumes such as Richman's *Many Rāmāyaṇas: The Diversity of a Narrative Tradition in South Asia* (and its forthcoming sequel *Questioning Rāmāyaṇas*), Thiel-Horstmann's *Rāmāyaṇa and Rāmāyaṇas*, and Brockington's massive recent study of both of the great Sanskrit epics.[2]

During the same period the public's fascination with the epic tale of Śrī Rāma, always profound, was further enhanced

---

1. These traditional verses in praise of Vālmīki are frequently recited by expounders of the *Rāmāyaṇa* tale and are commonly prefaced to manuscripts and printed editions of Sanskrit commentaries on the poem.
2. See appended bibliography for references.

by Doordarshan's broadcasts of Ramanand Sagar's enormously popular serial *Rāmāyaṇ* and its subsequent dissemination in India, other parts of Asia, and throughout the South Asian Diaspora in the form of video cassettes. This last version, to which I shall have occasion to refer again, is noteworthy in the present context for its author's efforts — in his video introduction to the series — to suggest that his version somehow incorporates elements of virtually all major Indian literary versions. This claim is addressed, one may note in passing, from a radically different perspective in Romila Thapar's well-known essay[3] in which she expresses the fear that Sagar's lowest common denominator serial might ultimately eclipse the folk and regional versions that lend such vibrancy and diversity to the *Rāmāyaṇa* tradition.

One curious and recurrent thread running through the fabric of these recent *Rāmāyaṇa* studies is a revisionist emphasis upon what are represented as non-hegemonic or counter-hegemonic versions of the epic story. This concern most often manifests itself in an effort to balance or counteract what is represented as a tendency among scholars to 'privilege' certain versions of the *Rāmāyaṇa* over others. We see this especially in the case of versions of the *Rāmakathā* that are regarded as literary rather than oral or 'folk' renderings. For such versions are frequently represented as embodying elitist, patriarchal and generally regressive social and political values unlike allegedly 'populist', 'subaltern', or 'feminist' retellings of the epic story.

This trend in *Rāmāyaṇa* scholarship is a reflection of relatively recent developments in the what is generally called Cultural Studies, a field that focuses our attention on relations of power in the areas of post-colonial Studies, Subaltern

3. Thapar, 1989

History, Gender Studies and so on and seeks to let the voices of less empowered sectors of society be heard, often in contestation of the more powerful and hegemonic voices of traditional elites. This trend is, I believe, largely a healthy one since it opens up to scholarly inquiry significant areas of humanistic research that have often been overlooked, ignored or even despised by scholars.

None the less, there are areas — and I believe that *Rāmāyaṇa* studies has been one of them — where in their righteous zeal to highlight areas of cultural production that have hitherto been kept in the background, some scholars have tended to inaccurately represent the nature and significance of the so-called 'elitist' renderings. In so doing they have also drawn too sharp a distinction between them and the supposedly more populist versions that form the focus of their own studies. This trend has given rise in turn to a certain ambivalence towards such literary *Rāmāyaṇa*s as the *Rāmcaritmānas* of Goswāmī Tulasī Dās and, especially, Vālmīki's Sanskrit *Ādikāvya*.

Thus several authors in some of the collections mentioned above repeatedly stress their intention not to 'privilege' Vālmīki. The reason for this, in the case of those scholars whose research has been largely focused on what they view as 'contestatory' *Rāmāyaṇa*s, that is to say, those thought to have been produced and/or consumed by women, backward caste groups, folk poets and popular performers, is that Vālmīki has come to be perceived as the very personification of precisely the sort of patriarchal, Brāhmaṇical, literate pan-Indian elitism that has become an object of scorn among many post-orientalist students of Indian culture.

This issue comes most clearly to the fore when such scholars attempt to summarise the Rāma story for their readers and find themselves — often reluctantly — forced to provide a synopsis of the *Vālmīki Rāmāyaṇa* as the most 'normative' version of the tale. Let me give a few examples. Paula Richman, in her introduction to the volume of *Rāmāyaṇa* studies she recently edited, presents Vālmīki's version 'not as an *Ur*-text but only as the story of Rāma with which the majority of Western *Rāmāyaṇa* scholars are most familiar. My goal is not to privilege Vālmīki's *Rāmāyaṇa*. . . .' (p. 5) In the same collection the late Professor Ramanujan calls Vālmiki's version, 'the earliest and most prestigious of them all'. (p. 25) Frank Reynolds complains that, 'The tendency unduly to privilege Hindu versions in general, and certain Hindu versions in particular, is evidenced by the common practice of referring to the various tellings of the Rāma story by the essentially Hindu term *Rāmāyaṇa*'. (p. 60) Kathleen Erndl in her comparative study of Vālmīki's and Kampan's treatments of the episode of the mutilation of Śūrpaṇakhā similarly assures us that, 'My intention is not to privilege it (Vālmīki's version) as the normative or *Ur*-text. . . .' (p. 68) Far from retaining his increasingly unenviable reputation as the very paragon of elitism and Brāhmaṇical privilege, it appears that the First Poet is suddenly at risk of joining the ranks of the seriously underprivileged.

In a similar vein, other authors are at pains to indicate that one element or another in the particular version of the *Rāmāyaṇa* they have chosen to study is not to be found in Vālmīki. Thus V. Narayana Rao in his interesting study of women's *Rāmāyaṇa* songs in Telugu writes of songs that 'tell a *Rāmāyaṇa* story very different from the familiar one attributed to Vālmīki'. (p. 114)

From these and other such comments scattered throughout much of recent *Rāmāyaṇa* scholarship one derives a sense that Vālmīki remains a kind of *eminence grise* for students of oral, folkloric, and 'contestatory' versions of the tale, a ghostly presence whom, despite their best and most politically correct intentions, these contemporary scholars cannot seem fully to exorcise. Ironically, it often seems that these scholars do indeed tend to 'privilege' Vālmīki's poem despite their protestations to the contrary by constantly setting it up as the norm against which all other versions are, in the end, contrasted. Not infrequently, moreover, scholarly comparisons of regional and folk *Rāmāyaṇas* with the monumental poem of Vālmīki seem but poorly informed about the history, nature, substance, and even contents of the latter.

In the light of this recent resurgence in interest in *Rāmāyaṇa* studies, I should like to speak up in defense of this spectral Vālmīki and his *Rāmāyaṇa* and try to situate them within the broader context of the Rāma legend and its cultural-historical trajectory.

None of this is to suggest that the Ādikavi has been without his defenders. Although, as we have seen, it has become distinctly unfashionable to 'privilege' a figure who is represented in some scholarly circles as the virtual poet laureate of high-caste, patriarchal, Brāhmaṇical culture, the culture of *varṇāśrama-dharma* as it is codified by authors such as Manu, some informed but non-academic writers have challenged the current scholarly trend in lay publications that are perhaps rarely read by Indologists.

Consider the following excerpt from such a source which, given the class and gender politics within which much of the current discussion of Vālmīki is framed, may seem as an unlikely one given Vālmīki's reputation as one of the pillars of the patriarchy. It is from a relatively recent number of the well-known Indian progressive women's journal *Mānuṣī;* and it is, in fact, a review of Richman's collection, *Many Rāmāyaṇas,* mentioned above. Responding to the stated intention on the part of so many of Richman's contributors not to privilege certain Hindu versions of the epic story, the author, Ruth Vanita, one of the co-founders of *Mānuṣī*, remarks:

> In the process, however, they implicitly and explicitly privilege Buddhist and Jain over Hindu versions, oral over written versions, and so-called 'people's' versions over texts attributable to an individual author. They have a general tendency to see the former in each of these pairs as more progressive, flexible and freedom-oriented.
>
> These preferences largely derive from the currently fashionable deconstructionist tendency for decanonisation. For instance, in their desire to 'offset the prevalent attitudes to Vālmīki,' some contributors [feel] that this well-established prevalent attitude may have something to do with poetic excellence. To say that Vālmīki's telling is merely 'one among many' is to overlook the time factor — the earliest extant version is likely to have been more influential than later versions.
>
> Instead of viewing differences as representing polar opposites, . . . these differences could be seen as part of the tradition's self-reflexiveness. Overlooking this important feature of the tradition results in simplistic readings and in self-contradiction as, for instance, saying that "men labeled 'low-caste'. . . have created and maintained counter-*Rāmāyaṇas*, when Valmiki himself was a member of one of the 'lowest' castes and is widely recognized as such by all castes. If the most privileged text was composed by a member of a

low caste, then what were the counter-*Rāmāyaṇas* countering?"[4]

Smt. Vanita's remarks about Vālmīki's low caste affiliation refer, of course, to the popular tradition current among many in India and especially so among those of traditionally low social status according to which the apparently brāhmaṇa sage turned poet, whom some traditions assign to the Bhārgava *gotra,* was actually of lowly birth and a 'bad character', a dacoit, into the bargain.[5] The literary locus classicus of this biographical information is the fifteenth- or sixteenth-century *Adhyātma Rāmāyaṇa,* a text included in the *Brahmāṇḍa Purāṇa,* which tells the story somewhat differently. According to this version Vālmīki was in fact a brāhmaṇa by birth (*janmamātradvijatvam*) who had become degraded through his having been raised by and among *kirāta*s and his having adopted the practices of śūdras. He becomes a highwayman and a murderer. Once, having accosted the *saptarṣi*s in order to rob them, he is asked by his victims why he has turned to a life of crime. He replies that he has done so as a means of supporting his (śūdra) wife and children. He is then directed by the seers to inquire of his family whether or not in addition to his spoils they are willing to share the sin he incurs in acquiring them.

The bandit complies and is shocked to learn that the answer is a resounding 'No!'. Realising the error of his ways, the outlaw repairs once more to the seers who advise him to purge himself of sin by sitting immobile for endless years muttering the *mantra marā, marā* (an inversion of the name of Rama). He does so and after the passage of thousands of eons, he is called forth from the large anthill or termite mound (*valmīka*) that has formed around his motionless body. It is this metaphoric

4. Vanita, 1993:37.
5. Goldman, 1976: 97-101

and spiritual rebirth that provides him with his most common name or epithet which we understand to be a mock patronymic Vālmīki, 'son of the anthill', a name similar to the epithet Dvaipāyana, 'son of the island' that is given to his fellow epic poet, Vyāsa. With a heart overflowing with *Rāmabhakti* as a result of his having repeated the holy *Rāmanāma* innumerable times, he is spiritually prepared to compose his monumental literary version of the *Rāmacarita*.[6]

This charming legend is no doubt a relatively late addition to the *Rāmāyaṇa* tradition, borrowing its theme of the sinner transformed through repetition of the Holy Name from the common medieval Vaiṣṇava *bhakti* topos and, most likely, even its most striking narrative motif, that of the *tapasvin* enclosed in an anthill, from the *Mahābhārata*'s version of the story of the Bhārgava *muni* Cyavana, whom some sources regard as a relative of Vālmīki, and his marriage to Sukanyā.[7]

The motif associated with this legend that has perhaps most haunted the Indian imagination in the era of modernity is doubtless that of the outcaste made pure or, to put it in more contemporary terminology, of the *dalit* empowered, and even made venerable to those born of high caste. It is this theme that led to the adoption on the part of north Indian sweeper communities, under the tutelage of the Ārya Samāj, to adopt Vālmīki as their eponymous spiritual forefather in the nineteenth century. Moreover, it is the power of this motif, and its significant socio-political implications that lay at the heart of the recent dispute over the omission and subsequent production and broadcast of the 'Sītā-tyāg' episode of the Doordarshan serialisation of the *Rāmāyaṇa*. There the interests of two distinct groups — the *dalit* group calling itself 'Vālmīkis'

6. *Adhyātma Rāmāyaṇa*, 2.64-86.
7. *Mahābhārata*, 3.121-24.

or Balmiks and high caste Hindus associated with the VHP — were tied up with the different denouements of the epic narrative as presented in Vālmiki's Uttara Kāṇḍa and in the other great north Indian hegemonic *Rāmāyaṇa*, the *Rāmacaritmānas* of Goswāmī Tulsī Dās, respectively. This confrontation, emblematic of contemporary caste politics, played itself out as, in effect, a battle of *Rāmāyaṇa*s in which the *dalit* adherents of the legendary outcaste Vālmīki and the high caste[8] partisans of the brāhmaṇa poet Tulsī Dās were pitted against one another. Most worthy of note here is that, in the end, through a combination of agitation from below (the 'brooms down' strike of the Balmiks) and intervention from above (the courts advised by a panel of *Rāmāyaṇa* experts) the matter was resolved in favour of Vālmīki (and the Vālmīkis), one of the few figures in the long cultural history of South Asia with equal claim upon and appeal to both 'forward' and "backward' caste groups.

Now although Smt. Vanita's arguments regarding the *Vālmīki Rāmāyaṇa* are no doubt subject to a number of qualifications, there is no doubt that she is correct to call our attention to some of the positive reasons for the longevity, influence and unparalleled prestige of Vālmīki's poetic rendering of the Rāma story. One may protest against the 'privileging' of the *Vālmīki Rāmāyaṇa*; but one still has to account for it. The point here is that in very large measure the work comes by its 'privileging' honestly; not only through its reputation and hoary antiquity but through the general consensus on the part of its original audiences and the many generations that have followed them that the poem is outstanding, even unique, in its literary merit. For few poets in the history of world literature have taken so vast and grand

8. Represented by the Vishva Hindu Parishad or VHP.

a theme, rendered it in an idiom that is both simple and noble, and imbued this rendering with greater pathos.

It was not, after all, Western scholars who conferred the title of *Ādikavi* on the *ṛṣi* Vālmīki and thus validated his masterwork's claim to be the *parama kavīnām ādhāram,* the great source for all poets. These claims have been constantly reiterated by the greatest of India's poets and *alaṅkāra-śāstrins.* Even the incomparable Kālidāsa confesses that he would not have dared undertake so awesome a theme as the history of the Raghu lineage were it not for the fact that the path had already been prepared for him by the First Poet and his followers.

> *athavā kṛtavāgdvāre vaṁśe 'smin pūrvasūribhiḥ* ।
> *maṇau vajrasamutkīrṇe sūtrasyevāsti me gatiḥ* ॥[9]

> But a gateway in the form of poetic speech to this royal lineage has already been opened by the first poet. Thus my path will be like that of a thread through a gemstone already pierced by a diamond drill.

Even when the great authorities on poetics proposed new formulations to explain the essence of poetry, they took care to show that they do not differ from the intentions of the celebrated *ṛṣis* who composed the great epics of antiquity.

> *vālmīkivyāsamukhyāś ca ye prakhyātaḥ kavīśvarāḥ* ।
> *tadabhiprāyabāhyo'yaṁ nāsmābhir darśito nayaḥ* ॥[10]

---

9. *Raghuvaṁśa,* 1.4. It is worth noting that the commentator Mallinātha takes the plural literally rather than as a marker of respect, commenting — *pūrvaiḥ sūribhiḥ kavibhiḥ vālmīkādibhiḥ* । *kṛtavāgdvāre kṛtaṁ rāmāyaṇādiprabandharūpā yā vāk saiva dvāraṁ praveśo yasya tasmin* (By the early seers are meant Vālmīki and so on. The speech that constitutes the gateway or means of access is in the form of such compositions as the *Rāmāyaṇa,* etc.).

10. *Dhvanyāloka,* 3.19 (*kārikā*).

> I have not represented anything that is outside of the intentions of the illustrious poetic masters starting with Vālmīki and Vyāsa.

Nor was the prestige of Vālmīki confined to the poets and rhetoricians of the elite Sanskritic tradition. It is not at all uncommon for authors composing in regional languages to explicitly cite the *Ādikāvya* as their exemplar and its author their inspiration even when, as is often the case, they have evidently derived much of their thematic material from some other version. Thus, for example, Smith cites the claim of the Oriyā poet Maheśvaradāsa in the latter's *Ṭīkā Rāmāyaṇa* to the effect that,

> *mahākabi bālamīka yāhā pāi dhanya* ।
> *prākṛta bhāṣāre tāhā karili barṇana* ॥

> I related in the Prākṛt language as much of Vālmīki as I deem excellent.[11]

I shall return to a more detailed discussion of the aesthetics of the Vālmīki *Rāmāyaṇa* below.

Smt. Vanita's comment on the 'time factor', that is on the chronological priority of Vālmīki's version, must also be taken seriously. One does not have to be a Sanskrit chauvinist to appreciate the fact that in the absence of serious merit in the arguments of those who have championed such texts as the *Mahābhārata*'s *Rāmopākhyāna* and the Pāli *Dasaratha Jātaka*, Vālmīki's monumental poem must be accepted as the earliest version of the Rāma story of which we have any knowledge. Although earlier and parallel versions of the tale have been hypothesised, we have no evidence of their having actually existed. Moreover, the failure to trace convincingly later

---

11. Smith, 1988: 51.

regional and sectarian variants to such texts means that for all practical purposes we must accept the various recensions of Vālmīki as in some sense the ultimate *literary* source for all known versions.

Now if we are to think about the reasons for the longevity and the pervasive influence of Vālmīki's monumental epic over perhaps the last two and a half to three millennia, we might be tempted to think in terms of the poem's status as one of the central religious documents of Hinduism in general and of Vaiṣṇavism in particular. Then too, closely related to this is the way in which the text has been read as a kind of national epic; the story of Āryan or Hindu India's struggle against alien and menacing political forces represented in the narrative as the barbaric and fearsome *rākṣasas*, implacable foes of Brāhmaṇical culture and civilization. Such thought would surely have merit but would be useful only for roughly half of what we think to have been the life span of this work.

For, as Pollock has argued in a recent article,[12] the politicisation of the Rāma legend does not appear to be traceable any further back than the advent of Islam as a significant force on the subcontinent despite the fact that the tale had had a long and rich literary and representational history prior to that time. Moreover, Pollock suggests, the incultation of Rāma as a central divinity of Hindu temple worship also does not appear to be highly developed in India prior to the medieval period. Indeed to follow the logic of his observations, the theological and political valences of the Rāma legend are closely intertwined but develop as part of a complex response on the part of Hindu polities to the challenge posed by Islamic raiders and rulers only from around the twelfth century CE.

12. Pollock, 1993: 261-97.

From that period on there is ample evidence, both in the development of significant temple cults of Rāma and in the plethora of mappings of the *Rāmakathā*, particularly the hero-*avatāra* as the saviour of Brāhmaṇical society and culture from the depredations of the *rākṣasas*, onto the various historical moments — medieval, Mughal, colonial, and post-colonial — at which groups positioning themselves as standing for a Hindu majority feel themselves besieged, dominated, or threatened by forces that are perceived as exogenous and alien. Indeed such representations of this element of the *Rāmāyaṇa* theme have become commonplace from the time of the Marāṭhī *Rāmdās Rāmāyaṇa* in which the Mughals occupy the role of the demons to the contemporary stump rhetoric of militant Hindu firebrands like Uma Bharati and Sadhvi Ritambhara who assign this role to the Indian Muslim population at large and invoke Rāma's pledge, as represented by Tulsī Dās, to rid the earth of demons to sanctify the Hindu Right's call for their subjugation or expulsion.

But the history of the *Rāmāyaṇa* in pre-Islamic India — or at least what we know of this history — appears to be rather different. Despite its role as a paradigmatic vehicle for the Vaiṣṇava doctrine of the *avatāra*, of the intervention of the Divine into cosmic and human history and its thematisation in temple friezes at least from the period of the Kailāsanātha temple at Ellorā, the Rāma legend itself does not appear to have formed the subject of any sustained discourse in religious philosophy or theology prior the time of Rāmānuja. Sectarian commentaries on Vālmīki's text, although they become relatively numerous in the late medieval and early modern periods, do not, so far as we know, seem to have been produced earlier than the twelfth century. Compare this with the *Bhagavad Gītā*, surely a later text than the core of the Vālmīki

Rāmāyaṇa, which becomes the subject of an elaborate religious and philosophical commentarial tradition as early as the seventh century CE.

Then too, up until the medieval and later periods which witness a virtual explosion of Sanskritic and regional devotional *Rāmāyaṇa*s from such works as the *Ānanda* and *Adhyātma Rāmāyaṇa*s in Sanskrit to the better and less well known Vaiṣṇava, *rasika* and Śākta renditions in virtually all of the regional literary languages of the subcontinent, the *Rāmāyaṇa* story can hardly be called the exclusive property of Hinduism. The legend was appropriated by Buddhists at least from the time of the compilation of the *Jātaka*s while Vālmīki's poem was known to and admired by the great early Buddhist poet Aśvaghoṣa. Jain authors especially made the Rāma legend their own, regarding Rāma not, of course, as an *avatāra* of Godhead, but as one of the thirty-two *śalākā-puruṣa*s, or exemplary Jain laymen and the hero of numerous Jain *Rāmāyaṇa*s. Indeed the popularity of the story and its hero is by no means limited to the indigenous cultures and religious traditions of South Asia as the *Rāmāyaṇa* comes to stand among the central and most influential cultural artefacts of a wide variety of Buddhist and Islamic nations of West and South-East Asia.

If then the *Rāmāyaṇa* cast so relatively slender a shadow on the religious and political life of Hindu India in the pre-Islamic period, how then are we to explain the durability of the work during the period of at least a millennium between its composition and its appropriation by the elite actors within these two critical arenas? Put another way, the question might be, what is it that kept the *Rāmāyaṇa* alive for the various religious and regional sub-cultures of South Asia and positioned it all but uniquely to bear the burdens of the theological and nationalistic demands that would later be placed upon it?

The answer to this question is to be found, it would seem, in two quite different spheres in which the poem of Vālmīki and its central thematic have loomed large from at least the beginning of the first millennium CE. These are the aesthetic and the didactic.

First the aesthetic: Vālmīki's place, and that of the monumental epic poem ascribed to him are absolutely unique within the realm of Sanskrit poetry and poetics. For if they are not universally regarded as the best that the tradition has to offer, they are — as noted above — nearly unanimously regarded as the first. The poem, as it has come down to us, is provided with a prologue (*upodghāta*) in the form of a celebrated metapoetical narrative which tells how the sage Vālmīki, moving through a sequence of transformative personal experiences, the first edifying, the second emotive, and the third inspirational, is able to fuse them into the production of a new medium of expression, the poetic. This characterisation of Vālmīki as the First Poet or Ādikavi and his *Rāmāyaṇa* as the First Poem or *Ādikāvya* appears to have gained an acceptance that was both early and widespread so that at least as early as the era of the celebrated Buddhist poet Aśvaghoṣa[13] in the first or second century CE. From at least that time onwards poets and rhetoricians writing in Sanskrit and non-Sanskritic languages alike begin to offer conventional forms of homage to Vālmīki whom they see as standing at the head of the lineage of poets.

Clearly the accomplishment of Vālmīki is one that the literary culture regards as foundational although, since the

13. *Buddhacarita*, 1.43: *vālmīkir ādau ca sasarja padyam.*

episode has received little detailed analysis from this perspective, it is not easy to say in exactly what ways the *Rāmāyaṇa* was seen to be sharply differentiated from the textual milieu (the genre of *itihāsa-puruṣa*) from which it emerged. Nonetheless it seems clear, both from the *upodghāta* and later discussions of the events it describes, that the creation of true *kāvya* is possible only when there is an equal blending of the didactic (content) and the aesthetic (form) and the whole is imbued with a sublimated form of powerful emotionality (*rasa*).

The *upodghāta* also seems to give great importance to the fact that the literary product thus engendered gains something of its claim to the title 'poetry' through the very fact that it is performable and appreciable by performers and audiences other than the poet whose own, unsublimated, emotions originally triggered its production.

> *samākṣarais caturbhir ya pādair gīto maharṣiṇā* ।
> *so'nuvyāharaṇād bhūtaḥ śokaḥ ślokatvam āgataḥ* ॥
> — 1.2.39

> The *śoka*, grief, that the great seer sang out in four metrical quarters, all equal in syllables, has, by virtue of its being repeated after him, become *śloka*, poetry.

Moreover, as the *upodghāta* goes on to state, the poem is particularly marked by its power as a performative, musical work which is imbued with all of the *rasa*s, the sublimated, aestheticised emotions posited by Bharatamuni and such later theoreticians of literary aesthetics as Ānandavardhana, Abhinavagupta, and Viśvanātha.

> *pādabaddho'kṣarasamas tantrīlayasamanvitaḥ* —1.2.17

> (It was) divided into metric quarters, equal in syllables, and suitable for the accompaniment of melodic and rhythmic instruments.

As taught to its legendary first performers, the singers Lava and Kuśa, and as performed by them, the epic is described with minute attention to the technical vocabulary of classical Indian vocal music:

> *pāṭhye geye ca madhuraṁ pramāṇais tribhir anvitam* ।
> *jātibhiḥ saptabhir yuktaṁ tantrīlayasamanvitam* ॥
>
> — 1.4.7

> It is sweet both when recited and when sung in the three tempos to the seven notes of the scale; and it is suitable for the accompaniment of melodic and rhythmic instruments.

Note too that along with the vocabulary of classical music we find, in the *upodghāta*'s description of the *Rāmāyaṇa*, what is perhaps the earliest appearance in a poetic text of the technical terminology associated with the *Nāṭyaśāstra* and *rasa-dhvani* school of *alaṅkāra-śāstra*:

> *rasaiḥ śṛṅgārakaruṇahāsyaraudrabhayānakaiḥ* ।
> *vīrādibhī rasair yuktaṁ kāvyam etad agāyatām* ॥
>
> — 1. 4.8

> The two of them (Lava and Kuśa) sang the poem, which is replete with all the poetic sentiments: the humorous, the erotic, the piteous, the wrathful, the heroic, the terrifying, and the rest.

Thus a major thrust of the *upodghāta* is to indicate that Vālmīki's contribution is principally one of form not substance and that his creation, the *Rāmāyaṇa*, also there called the *Paulastyavadha* and the *Sītācarita*,[14] was originally an oral performative[15] and

---

14. *Vālmīki Rāmāyaṇa*, 1.4.6 and note *ad loc.* in Goldman, 1985: 286.
15. Although Pollock in a recent essay (1995 : 112-42) offers the hypothesis that this may be a 'nostalgic fiction' of written culture.

musical piece. Deriving its power from its unique sublimation of emotion into art and from its ability to convey this emotionalised aesthetic experience through performance to an audience distanced in time and space from the events it describes, the poem became the great vehicle for the broad popular diffusion of the Rāma legend.

It should be clear, of course, that Vālmīki's *mahākāvya* is not to be seen as the 'original' version of the tale of Śrī Rāma. Indeed the poem itself explicitly excludes any such notion. Like the *Mahābhaārata*, the *Rāmāyaṇa* is not intended to be understood as a piece of fiction created from the fertile imagination of a bard, but rather as a poetic rendering of actual historical events. In fact, so far as the content of the narrative is concerned, the *ādikavi* is not represented as having created anything at all. On the contrary he is explicitly shown to have been first the audience of a terse and decidedly prosaic (though metrical) oral rendition of the tale of Rāma as narrated to him by *devarṣi* Nārada. Only then does he render that story, along with many additional incidents revealed to him through his divinely granted *pratibhā*, into the *ādikāvya*.

> *śrutvā vastu samagraṁ tad dharmātmā dharma-saṁhitam* ।
> *vyaktam anveṣate bhūyo yad vṛttam tasya dhīmataḥ* ॥
> — 1.3.1

> And so it came about that the righteous man, having learned the entire substance of that story, exemplary of righteousness, the tale of wise Rāma, sought to make it public.

Thus, although it may be transparently obvious to an Indian audience deeply steeped in the Rāma legend in at least one of its innumerable versions, the Western critic must be reminded that Vālmīki's reputation does not at all rest on his having created the Rāma story but rather on his having transformed a historical tale that — however uplifting and inspiring it may be — is merely a recounting of actual events, into a work of poetry and music, that appeals as powerfully to the senses and the emotions as to the intellect and spiritual faculties. In testimony of this we may note how, in discussing the *Rāmāyaṇa* songs composed and performed by Andhra brāhmaṇa women (who incidentally feel that Vālmīki's account of the events in the lives of Rāma and Sītā is not necessarily the 'correct' one), V. Narayana Rao has observed that,

> Like most of the participants in the tradition, these women believe the *Rāmāyaṇa* to be fact and not fiction, and its many different versions are precisely in keeping with this belief. Contrary to the usual opinion, it is fiction that has only one version; a factual event will inevitably have various versions, depending on the attitude, point of view, intent, and social position of the teller.[16]

On the basis of Vālmīki's undeniably artful integration of the substantive and the aesthetic, then, the text's prophecy that it would be a great source of inspiration for poets has largely been fulfilled. For indeed the work has served as the source and/or inspiration for countless oral, written, dramatic, and artistic texts in all of the classical and regional languages of the major Hindu, Buddhist, Jain and Islamic cultures of South and South-East Asia.

It did not, however, achieve this unparalleled status by virtue of its aesthetic charm alone; although it is true that few of the works it has inspired can rival it in poetic charm and power. It is here that one has to examine the nature of the

16. Narayana Rao, 1992: 115.

content of the *Rāmāyaṇa*, once again quite apart from its theological and nationalist readings mentioned above, to try to understand its duration, pervasiveness and influence.

Vālmīki's putative source, the oral narrative of Rāma's career, related to him by the divine seer Nārada makes no explicit reference to theology or indeed to any cosmic or even 'national' mission of its hero. It is the story of an unusually virtuous prince, endowed with all the virtues of an Āryan aristocrat of the Vedic age who willingly foregoes his royal inheritance in deference to a vow of his father and cheerfully accepts a life of exile and penury rather than assert his own claims against the powerful societal norms of subordination to senior males and to the abstract principles of truth (*satya*) and righteousness (*dharma*). In exile, he suffers the agony of the abduction of his beloved wife, but exhibits exemplary fortitude and perseverance, mounting a successful military campaign to recover her and punish her abductors. He then resumes his rightful throne and ushers in a utopian age of peace, order and prosperity before ascending, after many years to the highest heaven.

What Nārada's text gives us and Vālmīki's expands and embellishes is the classical and never superseded idealised representation of the normative South Asian personality, powerful, compassionate, lovable and learned, capable of commanding nations and contesting even the gods, but always ready to renounce his own interests and desires in favour of those of the social and ritual order. Rāma is, above all, a prodigy of self-control, of the mastery of the ego and the senses and of the subordination of the interests of the individual to the demands of the socius. In Freudian terms he is a living example of the triumph of the superego over the id and as such has become the standard model for social behaviour for countless generations, the radical opposite of his demonic counterpart, the monstrous *rākṣasa* tyrant, Rāvaṇa, a grotesque caricature of unbridled self-indulgence and contempt for legitimate authority.

It is this characterisation, surely, and not his status for Vālmīki and the Hindu tradition as an *avatāra* of Viṣṇu, that has led Buddhist, Jain, and later, Muslim authors to adapt the Rāma legend to their own purposes in order to make him an exemplar of the Buddhist virtues of self-control in the *Dasaratha Jātaka* and the Thai *Ramakian*, the ideal practitioner of *ahiṁsā* in the Jain *Rāmāyaṇa*s, and the ideal of the resourceful Islamic prince in the wayang dramas of the Malay-Indonesian world, respectively.

In addition to the towering figures of Rāma and Rāvaṇa, Vālmīki has peopled his epic with a variety of characters who are themselves powerfully exemplary of normative and counter-normative roles in traditional South Asian society. Thus Vālmīki's Sītā is crafted as a figure to be held up to this day as the model for Hindu wifehood while Lakṣmaṇa has become the archetype of the deferential and devoted follower whom all younger siblings should try to emulate. Similarly, Kaikeyī has become proverbial as the insubordinate or shrewish wife, the dreaded figure who, as the modern idiom has it, 'eats her husband'.

It is these qualities, then, on the one hand the powerful aesthetic resonance of Vālmīki's poetry and the enormous prestige it gained for him as the First Poet and, on the other hand, the unparalleled didactic quality of his tale and his characterisations that sustained and expanded the power and influence of the *Rāmāyaṇa* during the first millennium of its life. Towards the end of that period the complex and intertwined political and religious history of the region, with the rise and spread of *bhakti* and temple worship as the dominant modes of Hindu religiosity and the advent of the powerful and unassimilable forces of Islam as significant political actors in the subcontinent, the tale becomes re-valorized, as it were, in ways that begin to foreground its 'latent' themes of the *Rāmāvatāra* and the notion of a divine hero whose mission would be the conquest and expulsion of 'demonic' aliens and the restoration of a prelapsarian Hindu utopia, the Rāmrāj.

Through this analysis, I believe, it is possible to shed light on what appears to be the two histories of the *Rāmāyaṇa* in general and Vālmīki's *Ādikāvya* in particular. Although all four of the themes of the Rāma legend are fully present at all stages of its history, it would appear that two, the aesthetic and the didactic are foregrounded in the earlier, pre-Islamic period while the other two, the devotional and the 'nationalistic', emerged into the foreground with the advent of Islam and have re-emerged in the past decade with the resurgence of communal politics in the Republic of India. This might, for example, help explain the enormous prestige and privileging of the *Vālmīki Rāmāyaṇa* for the first millennium of its life and its relative occlusion by versions emphasising the theological and the political, versions such as those of Rām Dās and, above all, Tulsī Dās in the later period.

Thus, the haunting presence of the enigmatic Vālmīki, the ghostly anthill sage, as felt in the long and pervasive influence of his monumental poetic masterpiece illustrates for us the fascinating ways in which a central cultural touchstone may serve, over time, the shifting needs and concerns of a great civilization which is as dynamic as it is conservative.

For far from being a textbook case of an unchanging and immemorial artefact of a culture supposedly insulated from the forces of historical change, the *Rāmāyaṇa* in its long survival through many shifts, changes, and upheavals in the life of South Asia, may be seen to provide, instead, in the history of its multiple readings, a unique yardstick wherewith to measure these metamorphoses.

Thus, in many ways, the great epic has lived up to the promise the creator divinity, Brahmā, made to the anthill sage:

yāvat sthāsyanti girayaḥ saritaś ca mahītale ।
tāvad rāmāyaṇakathā lokeṣu pracariṣyati ॥

yāvad rāmasya ca kathā tvatkṛtā pracariṣyati ।
tāvad ūrdhvam adhaś ca tvaś mallokeṣu nivatsyasi ॥
— 1.2.35-36

As long as the mountains and rivers remain upon the earth the story of the *Rāmāyaṇa* will remain current among the people.

And as long as the story of Rāma that you composed shall remain current, you shall live on in my worlds, above and below.

Bibliography

Brockington, John., *Righteous Rāma: The Evolution of an Epic*, Delhi: Oxford University Press, 1984.

———, *The Sanskrit Epics*, Brill: Leiden, 1998.

The Buddhacarita or Acts of the Buddha, Lahore. Complete Sanskrit Text with English Translation (Cantos I-XIV translated from the original Sanskrit supplemented by the Tibetan version together with an introduction and notes). Ed. E.H. Johnston, 1936, rpt. Delhi, Motilal Banarsidass, 1972.

Dhvanyāloka of Ānandavardhana, Bombay: Nirṇayasāgar Press. With the Locana commentary of Abhinavagupta, ed. Durgāprasād and Kāśīnāth Pāṇḍurang Parab, 1891.

Goldman, Robert P., ed., *The Rāmāyaṇa of Vālmīki: An Epic of Ancient India*, 5 vols, Princeton: Princeton University Press, 1984-96.

———, 'Vālmīki and the Bhṛgu Connection', *Journal of the American Oriental Society*, vol. 96, no.1, 1976, pp. 97-101.

Hart, George L. and Hank Heifetz, trans. and eds., *The Forest Book of the Ramayana of Kampan*, Berkeley: University of California Press, 1988.

Lutgendorf, Phillip, *The Life of a Text: Performing the Ramcaritmanas of Tulsidas*, Berkeley: University of California Press, 1991.

Mahābhārata: Critical Edition (1933-70), 24 vols., Poona: Bhandarkar Oriental Research Institute. With Harivaṁśa Critically ed. V.S. Sukthankar, *et al.*, 1969-71.

Narayana Rao, V., 'A *Rāmāyaṇa* of their Own: Women's Oral Tradition in Telugu'. In Richman, Paula, ed., *Many Rāmāyaṇas: The Diversity of a Narrative Tradition in South Asia*, Berkeley: University of California Press, 1992, pp. 114-36.

Pollock, Sheldon, '*Rāmāyaṇa* and Political Imagination in India', *Journal of Asian Studies*, 52.2, (May 1993), pp. 261-97.

———, 'Literary History, Indian History, World History', *Social Scientist*, 23.10-12, 1995. pp. 112-42.

Raghuvaṁśa of Kālidāsa, with commentary *Sañjīvanī* of Mallinātha; extracts from the commentaries of Vallabhadeva, Hemādri, Dinkara Misra Charitavardhan, Sumativyaya (Raghuvaṁśasāra); critical and explanatory notes, various readings, and indexes. With an introduction by H. D. Velankar, Bombay: Nirṇayasāgar Press, 1948.

The Vālmīki Rāmāyaṇa: Critical Edition, 7 vols., Baroda: Oriental Institute, General ed. G.H. Bhatt and U.P. Shah, 1960-75.

Richman, Paula, ed., *Many Rāmāyaṇas: The Diversity of a Narrative Tradition in South Asia*, Berkeley and Los Angeles: University of California Press, 1992.

———, *Questioning Ramayanas: A South Asian Tradition*, Delhi: Oxford University Press and Berkeley: University of California Press, 1999.

Smith, W.L., *Rāmāyaṇa Traditions in Eastern India: Assam, Bengal, Orissa*, Stockholm: Department of Indology, University of Stockholm, 1988.

Thapar, Romila, 'The Ramayana Syndrome', *Seminar* 353, 1989.

Thiel-Horstmann, Monika, ed., *Rāmāyaṇa and Rāmāyaṇas*, Wiesbaden: Otto Harrassowitz, 1992.

Van der Veer, Peter, *Gods on Earth: The Management of Religious Experience and Identity in a North Indian Pilgrimage Centre*, London: The Athlone Press, 1988.

Vanita, Ruth, 'We Make it Better', *Mānuṣī*, no. 78., 1993, Sept-Oct. 1993.

2

Images of Women in the Prambanan Rāmāyaṇa Reliefs

Alessandra Lopez y Royo

Abstract

THE beautifully carved *Rāmāyaṇa* reliefs of the Loro Jonggrang temple at Prambanan in Central Java (*circa* ninth century CE), are evidence of the popularity of this story in the ancient Javanese world. This paper attempts to look at the way the feminine is represented in these reliefs. The analysis will consider iconographic conventions used by the sculptors as well as the iconology of the reliefs. This involves looking, for comparison and supporting evidence, at the way women are portrayed in the Old Javanese *Rāmāyaṇa Kakawin*. The analysis will focus on matters of style and composition, highlighting where appropriate correspondences and discrepancies between the literary and sculptural interpretation of the story and pointing out links with performance, which can be inferred from the conventions of body representation and from the development of the narrative. The analysis will then move on to examine the female experience as seen in the reliefs. This will be arranged in a cluster of themes, retrievable from the narrative : power, chastity, marriage, seduction, motherhood and spirituality. The focus will be on the models and patterns of behaviour revealed by the narrative. Though the Javanese interpretation of the *Rāmāyaṇa* cannot provide us, for obvious reasons, with a faithful account of the position and role of women in ancient Javanese society, the narrative does constitute evidence of how the feminine was construed and perceived within the culture of that period. Such factors should be taken into account when investigating the cultural history of the Indonesian islands.

Introduction

Built in the ninth century CE — the exact date is uncertain — the Prambanan temple complex is one of the largest in Java. The very area in which the complex is found is rich in temple art, with Buddhist temples and Hindu ones erected at a relatively short distance from one another. This gives an indication of the religious climate of Central Java in the ninth century. Jordaan goes as far as conjecturing that Prambanan itself was a Hindu-Buddhist collaborative effort (1993), highlighting the religious tolerance of this period of Javanese history.

No doubt Prambanan is one of the largest Śaiva temple complexes ever built outside India. It is made up of concentric courts, measuring respectively 390 × 390 metres (outside yard), 222 × 222 metres (middle yard) and 110 × 110 metre (inner yard). The outer and middle yard were once surrounded by hundreds of small temples now in ruins. In the middle of the principal court (inner yard) there are three temples, the central one dedicated to Śiwa, the other two to Wiṣṇu and Brahmā.[1] The inner yard contains altogether 8 temples (Subarno 1991:16-18).

---

1. In this paper Old Javanese words are spelt in Roman following the entries in Zoetmulder's Old Javanese- English Dictionary (1982). Since much of the vocabulary of Old Javanese is of Sanskrit origin, it may sometimes appear that Sanskrit words are being transliterated erroneously. Sometimes the spelling coincides with that used in standard transliterations from Sanskrit, sometimes it does not. There is nothing I can do about such discrepancies, short of devising another →

The *Rāmāyaṇa* reliefs, already the object of numerous studies — most notable among them that of Stutterheim (1987), Kaelan (1963) and, more recently, Levin (1996)[2] can be seen around the inner balustrade of the Śiwa and Brahmā temple. The reliefs tell the story of prince Rāma, beginning with the gods requesting Wiṣṇu to help, continuining with the major events prior to Rāma's exile in the forest and then going on to narrate the war with Rāwaṇa, following Sītā's abduction by him. The narrative continues with the rescue of Sītā, her banishment and then with the story of Lawa and Kuśa, the two sons of Rāma and Sītā.

I will not focus on the narrative sequence of the reliefs, which is very well known through the writings of the above-mentioned authors. The story as told in the reliefs does not seem to follow closely any known literary version of the Rāma story, though it is not too dissimilar from Vālmīki's. This seemed to have caused much anxiety to many scholars, who believed that narrative sculpture must follow a literary text and tried to find reasons why this should be so. Even though opinions often varied quite considerably in terms of identification of the text which had been used, there has been, by and large, consensus on the notion that the reliefs must depend on a written text.

Thus, it was acceptable in the past to talk of deviations from Vālmīki's text as due either to ignorance of Sanskrit which prevented the sculptors from an adequate rendering of the

→ transliteration system, which I am not convinced would solve the problem. I must point out however that in the context of classical Indonesia it makes more sense to use the Old Javanese romanised spellings, regardless of whether a word has an Indonesian or a Sanskrit origin and this is the principle I have followed throughout the paper, *pace* all Sanskritists.

2. Jordaan in 1995 mentioned a forthcoming study by Jan Fontein but I have not yet seen it (Jordaan 1995:4).

textual material or reliance on some lost Javanese text or on a version based on Vālmīki's text which is different from the texts now extant in India, since the Old Javanese *Rāmāyaṇa* (*OJR*) *Kakawin* does not seem to have a direct link with the reliefs, though one should note that Vālmīki's *Rāmāyaṇa* and the *Kakawin* are relatively close.[3] The main difference between the *Kakawin* and the reliefs is in the complete omission of the Lava and Kuśa story in the *Kakawin*, which ends with the trial of Sītā by fire and general rejoycing in Ayodhyā following the event, whereas the reliefs skip Sītā's trial by fire and go on to the Lawa and Kuśa episodes.

Work done by art historians on the way narrative sculpture relates to literary texts has highlighted the fact that it cannot be expected that a story told through a visual medium would be identical with its literary version (Klokke 1993; Sedyawati 1993). The interpretation in sculpture follows its own narrative conventions and sculptors use their own devices to show, for example, the unfolding of events through time. Most of all, a story retold in the medium of sculpture often simply acts as a reminder. Some transitional episodes may be skipped, others may be elaborated upon, enriched with details deriving from daily life. The sculptor's assumption is that viewers will see a well-known story and recreate it in their own imagination. The visual material constitutes a reflection of core beliefs and simultaneously provides access to those beliefs. Stories are never told in a linear fashion, they are intended as an aid to meditation and visualisation.[4]

3. The main source for OJR is *Bhaṭṭikāvya Rāvaṇavadha* (The Slaying of Rāvaṇa). Khanna and Saran have recently suggested that the Old Javanese poet followed both Bhaṭṭi and Vālmīki (1993: 228).

4. I am particularly indebted to Susan Huntington for these insights on the relationship of texts and narrative reliefs. Huntington presented a series of lectures and seminars to discuss the problem of how texts →

Another important point is that stories such as the *Rāmāyaṇa* were in all likelihood enacted. A Javanese inscription going back to the ninth century refers to dramatic entertainment, and an inscription of the tenth century describes the enactement of the *Rāmāyaṇa* (Soedarsono 1984:3). It is therefore likely that oral transmission was a strong tradition which informed the dramatic rendering of the story, which in turn may have influenced visual representations of the narrative, particularly in terms of characterisation.

It has been repeatedly observed that the story of the *Rāmāyaṇa* is of Indian origin. What can it therefore tell us about the world of ancient Java? Though the story is undoubtedly of Indian origin, its rendering as found in Java, is not. If we accept that a visual interpretation is not tied to a written text but represents a rendering of the text or texts, the interpretation is bound to be significantly coloured by a local, in this case Javanese, perspective, particularly in terms of details of representation such as buildings, ornamentation, dress and, I would add, postures and expressions. If we then look at locally produced literary versions of the story, such as the Old Javanese *Rāmāyaṇa Kakawin*, it is a Javanese world which we encounter and this is apparent from the way the story is narrated, and from the so-called deviations from what is usually held to be the original *Rāmāyaṇa*, viz., the *Rāmāyaṇa* of Vālmīki.[5] Consequently we can look at how women are portrayed and imagined, in both literary and sculptural

---

→ and narrative reliefs relate to one another, particularly in the context of Buddhist art, while holding the position of Numata Visitor in Buddhist Studies at Balliol College, University of Oxford, Michaelmas term 1998. Some of her observations are, however, also applicable to Hindu art.

5. I would like to refer here to Richman (1991) where the notion of an authentic original text of the *Rāmāyaṇa* is challenged and the diversity of the *Rāmāyaṇa* tradition, seen as multivocal, is explored.

versions from Java and see through this how the Javanese interpreted and construed the feminine.

Iconographic Conventions

Let us first look at the way women are portrayed in the reliefs: what actions do we see them perform? How do they stand or sit? In what way is the language of body postures and movements manipulated to represent them?

Sedyawati (1993) has already observed that women and men seem to have different sitting positions: in group scenes in which men and women are seen seated, the men have their legs crossed, whereas the women sit on their heels, in a position that is still used in Javanese court dance today, in *putri* style — as the women begin their *sembah* in a *srimpi* or *bedhoyo* dance. This convention of differentiated sitting positions is not observed in all scenes and sometimes the sitting-on-the heels position is not shown with the same degree of restraint, that is, the sitting posture is a little more relaxed and less defined, involving a slight turn of varying degrees for the torso. But in general it can be agreed that there seems to be a difference in the way men and women sit. On more careful observation, it can be suggested that this might reflect court practices, which are likely to have influenced the portrayal of the characters in the story.

Works from Majapahit times, such as *Nawanatya,* elaborate on court etiquette and give details of how the courtier should behave in the presence of the king, specifying the direction of the glance and so on. *Nawanatya* is thought to be linked with performance practices (Holt 1967:286). Manuals are usually codifications of practices already known and already established as tradition, thus even though *Nawanatya* is not contemporary with the reliefs, it nevertheless testifies to the existence of a tradition of court conventions and etiquette allied to those employed in dramatic performance for characterisation. The use of similar conventions in iconography further strengthens the suggestion of an interrelationship between the visual and performing arts, from a relatively early period, in ancient Java (cf. Sedyawati 1993).

Some female characters in the Prambanan *Rāmāyaṇa* are shown standing in stylised *tribhaṅga* postures, similar to those shown by *Widyādharīs* on the walls of other *caṇḍīs*. They often hold lotus stems or are surrounded by them, as seen next to one of Sītā's attendants in the relief in which the events leading to her marriage to Rāma are interpreted with a skillful use of body postures to convey a range of emotions. Here Sītā's head is slightly tilted to the left (right of the viewer), the body is in a *tribhaṅga*, her left hand is at the front of her body, below her breasts, in a stylised *kaṭakāmukha* gesture.[6] Her companions can also be seen in a related posture, but only Sītā's head is shown inclined — this is important as only with the inclination of the head one can form a perfect *tribhaṅga*, the position of the body being otherwise only a raising of the waist/hip, technically known as *udvāhita kaṭi*.[7]

6. Here I am using the terminology found in Sanskrit texts such as *Nāṭyaśāstra* to name and describe the hand gestures and the body postures seen in the reliefs. This is arbitrary but justifiable. The gestures match the descriptions given in the Sanskrit texts and there is ample evidence, through iconography, to allow us to propose that the dance and dramatic conventions of the *Nāṭyaśāstra* were well known in the dance and dramatic practice of ancient Java. We do not know what the Javanese technical terminology was but the use of Sanskrit technical terminology allows us to name what we see.

7. *kaṭi* refers to the waist /hip area and the word is usually translated as 'waist'. However, it is not the waist that is raised but the hip (and obviously the waist is also raised in the process). Thus I prefer to translate the term as hip.

The *tribhaṅga* is a quintessentially feminine stance. It is the standing posture of beautiful women, it has sensuousness though it is not explicitly erotic. The tilt of the head and the gaze coyly directed towards the ground capture the essence of Sītā's characterisation: a shy, young woman of high birth, of great beauty, displaying the restrained behaviour expected from women of her rank. The slenderness and elongation of her limbs emphasise the aesthetic preferences of the Javanese, for whom elongation of the limbs was associated with elegance and refinement and was also a sign of divinity, a feature that has been preserved in the fashioning of *wayang* (shadow) puppets and which is very apparent in the East Javanese style of iconography — and Sītā is divine, being a form of Śrī.

The *kaṭakāmukha* hand does not have a specific meaning but it is worth noting that the hands of the *apsarās* holding lotuses are always in *kaṭakāmukha* and by association a *kaṭakāmukha* hand is suggestive of lotuses and flower garlands.[8] Through the use of a technique of association to convey multiple meanings, the sculptor seemed to wish to emphasise the physical loveliness of Sitā by adorning her with imaginary lotuses, alluding to her fragrance through suggesting the fragrance of flowers. Her attendants are also shown to be beautiful and they too hold their hands in *kaṭakāmukha* in the background, a device used to emphasise a little composition within the composition — a beauty surrounded by beauties, with the attendants setting off the supreme beauty of Sītā.

It is appropriate to compare this figurative interpretation with some of the verses of the *Kakawin*. Levin (1996) has pointed out how the visual lexicon of Javanese sculptors shows acquaintance with and a relationship with the poetics of

---

8. In the *Nāṭyaśāstra* the *kaṭakāmukha* hand is said to be used to show flowers or flower garlands (*NS*, 9, 60-63).

Kakawin poetry, itself strongly influenced by Sanskrit *alaṁkāra* devices. Thus, in the passage in which Sītā pays obeisance to her father and her father-in-law, at the time of her wedding, the poet describes her as adorned and fragrant with flowers:

> *nā ling niromītu ta sang wara rājakanyā* ।
> *pahyas huwus hana kabeh masekar sugandha* ॥
> *mangsö manembah i sirang naranātha kālih* ।
> *lāwan sirang nrepatipūtra surāmabhadra* ॥

> Thus he spoke. The beautiful princess together with prince Surāmabhadra after being fully dressed and adorned with fragrant flowers, came forward to pay obeisance to the two kings.
>
> — *OJR* 2, 64 tr. Soewito Santoso 1980[9]

But the association of women and flowers goes further, the flowers are not just an adornment. They are deeply connected with a perception of female sexuality. When Rāwaṇa, disguised as a hermit, addresses Sītā in a later passage of the *Kakawin*, his words are:

> *ikana hayunta yāk inet-inet ya kadi pwa sekar* ।
> *huwus inisep nikang bhramara teka sari nyu rurū* ॥
> *hana ta hayu nya mātra kawekas ya paḍanta katon* ।
> *ya ta panenerkwawās ya sira siniwīnta hana* ॥

> As I look closely at your beauty to me it is like that of a flower which has already lost its honey to a honey bee and its pollen has fallen. There are still traces of

9. Soewito Santoso's translation of the *Rāmāyaṇa Kakawin* is somewhat controversial. Some scholars find that the translation does not do justice to the text and that the manuscript used is not wholly reliable in some places (S. Robson pers. comm; Kuntara Wiryamartana pers. comm). In the context of this paper, quoting from Santoso's work does not affect the main import of my argument. However, I would like readers to be aware of this issue.

its beauty apparent. You are like that. That is why I can see that you have a husband.

— *OJR* 5, 74 tr. Soewito Santoso 1980

Thus, in suggesting that the bride-to-be Sītā is surrounded by lotuses in full bloom the sculptor makes an allusion to her purity and her ripeness.

In a comparable manner, flowers play an important role in the episode of Śūrpaṇakhā's attempted seduction. The *rākṣasī* turns herself into a beautiful young woman seen in the relief as holding a lotus and with an *udvāhita* hip. Her gaze is directed at Rāma, thus she is making her desire explicit. This is contrary to all rules of refined and composed behaviour. Indeed in the *OJR Kakawin* Śūrpaṇakhā is described as very beautiful but her bold behaviour is greeted by Lakṣmaṇa with the words:

yuwatī kita kanyakā kuneng ।
adhawātah lakunta ta diṇḍara ॥
ya matang nya taman keneng irang ।
ta wuwus torasi ring hulun n ari ॥

You are a young lady and perhaps still a virgin, but you act like a widow, not like an innocent girl. That is why you are not shy and do not talk to me in a respectful way.

— *OJR* 4, 40, tr. Soewito Santoso 1980[10]

In the relevant relief we see a beautiful woman, richly adorned,

---

10. I am a little puzzled by this translation and by the text too. In Zoetmulder's dictionary the second verse is given as '*athawātah palakunta dindare*' where *palakunta* from *palaku* is 'request' and *dindare* is glossed as 'childish' (with a question mark) (Zoetmulder, 1982:405).

making an offering to Rāma. We see flowers as part of the offering. This is not Sītā, as suggested by some[11] but Śūrpaṇakhā herself. The flowers are normally part of any offering but here a double meaning is certainly intended. Śūrpaṇakhā is making sexual advances and the flowers hint at the situation.

Going on to another relief, we see Kekayī, the beloved queen of king Daśaratha, who insisted on having her son Bharata crowned king instead of Rāma, shown sitting close to her husband in a posture suggestive of intimacy and with the head close to that of the king, as if she were whispering in his ear. Her face is calm and restrained and one can imagine that her language too is refined and restrained, though the tense closeness of the figures brings out the intense drama. She is pointing at the collection of offerings and is possibly reminding her husband of his promise. Stutterheim comments on the fact that Kekayī's head is unadorned, a reference to her taking off her jewellery when she asked for her wish to be fulfilled, as described in Vālmīki's *Rāmāyaṇa* (Stutterheim 1987:151).

In the *Kakawin* Kekayī is described in a few verses when Daśaratha's queens are introduced:

> *Sang Kekayī Sumitrā Kośalyā ghara sang narendra tiga* ।
> *Durggā Gangā Gorī pada nira surūpa dibyaguṇa* ॥

> Kaikeyī, Sumitrā and Kośalyā . . . who in beauty and excellence equalled Durggā Gangā and Gorī
>
> — *OJR* 1, 17 tr. Santoso 1980

It is significant that Kekayī should be compared with Durgā, particularly in view of the known Śaivite allegiance of the

11. Stutterheim, however, thinks that this is Śūrpaṇakhā (Stutterheim, 1987:160)

Kakawin.[12] But here there is a further nuance of meaning. In ancient Java Durgā was seen as beautiful, powerful and warrior-like, the slayer of the demon Mahiṣa, an image that can be seen at Prambanan itself, in the north cella of *caṇḍī* Śiwa. The image is also known as Loro Jonggrang, from a legendary local princess and *caṇḍī* Śiva is often referred to by that name. But Durgā was also perceived as terrifying and frightening to behold, a demonic Bhairawī whose power was geared to destruction. Indeed Kekayī's actions will lead to the death of Daśaratha, hence the comparison is suggestive of uncontrolled power.

In the relief in which the coronation of Bharata is shown, there is a dance scene, in which a woman, holding a sword and a shield, performs a war dance. Stutterheim compares this figure to those of Tibetan *ḍākinī*s and suggests a Tāntric ceremonial dance (1987:153). This comparison is not out of place, in view of the strong Śaivite content of the *Rāmāyaṇa Kakawin* and the marked Tāntric character of Śaivism in ancient Java.[13] Here I wish to observe that in much later times, the courts of Surakarta and Yogyakarta used to maintain a corps of female bodyguards who were also skilled dancers. Perhaps this relief shows us the antecedents of this much later tradition.

---

12. Zoetmulder reports Poerbatjaraka's view that *OJR* is almost fanatically Śaivite (1974:233). cfr. *OJR Kakawin* 1, 7: 'Daśaratha was a faithful adherent of Śaiwism and conducted Śiwa worship regularly with increasing dedication' (*māheśwara ta sira lanā/ śiwabhakti ginön lanā ginawe*)' (tr. Soewito Santoso 1980) . On the Śaivism of *OJR*, see also Nihom 1996, in which he argues that *OJR* can throw light on the varieties of Śaivism of classical Indonesia.

13. There is also a long passage in *OJR Kakawin* which has a supposedly Tāntric flavour. It describes the physical union of Rāma and Sītā, after the fire ordeal, during the night following their return to Ayodhyā. Their lovemaking is symbolic of the mystical union of Śiva and Śakti. The *Kakawin* describes them as being deeply absorbed in meditation, contemplating the essence of the Supreme Truth (Santoso, 1980:33).

The woman dancer performs a dynamic, semi-acrobatic leap and exudes strength.

From such examples we can already see that the iconographic conventions show a link with perfomance in terms of body language and characterisation, as also with conventions exploited in *Kakawin* literature. One could continue to point out other such links with performance in details like the inward-bent elbows of refined characters, especially women, a sign of elegance and beauty one still observes in the tradition of Javanese court dance as it has come down to us and which, incidentally, shows a remarkable continuity of aesthetic conventions. There is an emphasis in the reliefs on refined behaviour. A character such as Sītā embodies court values and sets the standard for the refined behaviour and demeanor of high ranking women.[14] One cannot but reiterate that whereas the story is Indian, the stylistic conventions used in its visual rendering at Prambanan have a definite Javanese flavour. In the *Rāmāyaṇa* reliefs of Prambanan it is a Javanese Sītā we encounter, not an Indian one.

The Female Experience as Seen in the Rāmāyaṇa Reliefs

From the *Rāmāyaṇa* story we can retrieve a cluster of themes around which the female experience is arranged. These can all be associated with the character of Sītā who is at the centre of all issues concerning power (as *śakti*), chastity, marriage, motherhood and spirituality. Sītā, in other words, is a model to be followed and encompasses the whole of the female experience. Here again we have to contend with the question whether Sītā represents Indian values and norms or Javanese ones. But this perspective is wholly inadequate to carry out

14. Indeed Sītā becomes the prototype of the first queen in Javano-Balinese culture (Vickers, 1989:44).

an analysis. The situation is far more complex. The *Rāmāyaṇa* story originated in India, as has so often been pointed out, but its interpretation in Java is wholly Javanese. The reverence accorded to it, as indeed to other Indian stories which are the raw material for *Kakawin* composition, has been explained by Wallis as the result of being a means to recreate a distant world of Indian ancestors, gods and legendary heroes (1980). Thus, the Indian story lines become fully integrated in Javanese culture and can no longer be separated from it, as in the retellings they become the expression of that culture.

Sītā represents a powerful model of the feminine, an embodiment of the values of the court culture of ancient Java and constitutes an example of how the feminine is construed, in a normative way. Sītā embodies *śakti*, power. In her we see the association of 'positive' power, that is, power not geared to destruction, and physical beauty.

Sītā is *kasaktin* and is chaste, the model of the chaste royal wife. Chastity is a means to obtain power — this is why ascetics perform penances and abstain from sexual intercourse. To be effective, chastity must be steadfast. Loss of chastity affects one's *śakti*. The *Kakawin* focuses on the purification by fire, as a way of proving and reasserting Sītā's chastity, after she is rescued from Rāvaṇa's captivity. She emerges from the fire unscathed, her chastity confirmed. The fire changes into a golden lotus and Agni and Śiwa appear to dispel Rāma's doubts:

> *atha sāmpun awās sirār śuci* ।
> *sira sang śrī janakātmajenapi* ॥
> *parituṣṭa sirang raghūttama malawas tākadasih sunirmmala*

> Thus when the purity of Janakātmaja was clearly proven by the ordeal by fire. Raghūttama was

delighted. She was so long separated from her beloved and yet she was flawless.

— *OJR* 24, 203 trans. Soewito Santoso 1980

The trial by fire is omitted in the reliefs. In these, the story continues with the banishment of Sītā, after her pregnancy arouses suspicion. The absence of a relief showing the trial by fire is remarkable but this does not mean that the episode was not known. The reliefs seem to elaborate on the theme of loss of chastity and Sītā is shown as being wronged, later vindicated by her sons Lawa and Kuśa. It is thus the role of Sītā as mother that is privileged in the reliefs and motherhood is exalted as a supreme feminine value. This is beautifully conveyed in the relief in which Sītā is seen with one of her twins, the baby swaddled in very thick wraps, surrounded by her maids — though in exile and leading the life of an ascetic, Sītā is still a high ranking woman and cannot be portrayed without ladies-in-waiting.

Seduction does figure in the *Rāmāyaṇa* story in the episode of Śūrpaṇakhā changing herself into an *apsarā*-like figure in order to seduce Rāma and Lakṣmaṇa, an attempt which ends with her disfigurement — not seen in the reliefs. Seduction is a dominant theme in Old Javanese literature and sculptural art. The main function of *apsarā*s is that of seducing gods, mortal men and demons whenever fit. They play a pivotal role in controlling the *śakti* of ascetics by inducing them to break their vows of chastity. See for example the following description of the behaviour of ascetics, from *OJR* 25, 41 (in this instance the girls are human but the gist of the verses is the same):

dibya sirang ṛsi sādhaka sādhu ।
sādhana ning magawe hayun meman ॥
tona nireka nahan nirapēkṇa ॥

tar kagiwang sira ring suka wāhya ॥

> Though the sages see the beautiful girls they are indifferent to them. Their minds are not perturbed by physical enjoyment.
>
> — *OJR* 25, 41 transl. Soewito Santoso 1980

The theme of seduction and temptation as a practice of the *apsaris* does not necessarily have a negative connotation since seduction of males practising abstinence is a necessary way of checking their accumulation of power which might create an imbalance in the world. But the other side of the coin is adultery, which is seen as particularly unacceptable when committed by women, mortal and immortal alike, and is invariably punished. One can only think of how this theme is developed in later works, such as *kidung Sudamala,* shown on *caṇḍī* Sukuh, in which Durgā is changed into a horrendous creature on account of her adultery and will have to be exorcised by the hero Sadewa who will restore her to her former beauty. Adultery or fear of it is a dominant theme in the *Rāmāyaṇa* story, in its visual rendering and in the *Kakawin,* through Śūrpaṇakhā's attempt to involve Rāma in an adulterous relationship, through Rāvaṇa kidnapping Sītā, through the need to reestablish Sītā's purity in the eyes of the world, either through the fire ordeal (as in the *Kakawin*) or through the action of her two sons Lawa and Kuśa (as seen in the reliefs).

A further *Rāmāyaṇa* theme related to the female experience is that of spirituality. Once again Sītā embodies this aspect, through her *śakti,* her chastity and devotion. During her exile in the forest with her two children, in the hut of a hermit (Vālmīki himself), Sītā lives the life of an ascetic woman, though as seen earlier she continues to be portrayed with the paraphernalia of a noble woman. She becomes a model of female asceticism and spirituality and of exemplary motherhood. Implicitly the two life modes, asceticism and motherhood, are being connected in the reliefs, and motherhood itself is elevated to a spiritual plane.

Conclusions

The *Rāmāyaṇa* story in ancient Java takes on a Javanese identity in the way it is rendered. This is particularly the case in its sculptural representation, as seen in the Prambanan *Rāmāyaṇa* reliefs. The story is shown with an intermixture of elements, attitudes and behaviours taken from daily life and specific to the court culture of the time.

The story is Javanised, not so much in terms of changing the plot in any considerable measure[15] but in terms of choosing which episodes should be retold and/or represented, as an attempt to create a continuity with a mythical ancestral world, constantly recreated through the performance of the story, in a variety of media. Within this framework we can look at the way the feminine is construed in ancient Javanese culture, examining the values transmitted and examining the portrayal of women characters in the reliefs, with an eye to the *Kakawin* literary tradition.

The poetics of the Old Javanese *Rāmāyaṇa Kakawin* is that of a Javanese *Kakawin*, 'an exemplary *Kakawin*', as Hooykaas called it (1958),[16] following conventions derived from Indian

15. I must clarify that here I am specifically referring to the *OJR* and the reliefs. There are of course other Javanised versions of the story with new characters and accretions, which are however not coeval with the ones examined in this paper.

16. I am not necessarily endorsing Hooykaas' view of the *OJR* as *ādi kakawin*, contested by Zoetmulder among others (1974: 232), I am simply borrowing from the title of his book to emphasise the high esteem in which the *OJR* has been held throughout the centuries.

models but enriched and transformed to suit Javanese sensibilities. A reading of the *Kakawin* broadens the interpretative options available to us when 'reading' the reliefs: the picture we gather is complex and not unambiguous and engages us in a process of constant questioning for a deeper understanding of ancient Javanese culture.

Bibliography

Creese, H., 'Images of women and embodiment in Kakawin Literature' in V.C. Mackie, ed., *Disorientations: Embodiements of Women in Asian Cultural Form*, Wild Peony Press, 1998.

Holt, C., *Art in Indonesia: Continuities and Change*, Ithaca: Cornell University Press, 1967.

Hooykaas, C., *The Old-Javanese Rāmāyaṇa an Exemplary Kakawin as to Form and Content*, Amsterdam: N.V. Noord-Hollandsche Uitgevers Maatschappij, 1958.

Jordaan, R.E., *Imagine Buddha in Prambanan. Reconsidering the Buddhist Background of the Loro Jonggrang Temple Complex*, Leiden: Vakgroep Talen en Culturen van Zuidoost-Azie en Oceanie, Rijksuniversiteit te Leiden, Semaian 7, 1993.

———, 'The origin of the Rāma reliefs on candi Prambanan (Central Java, Indonesia)', Paper presented at the XIIth Rāmāyaṇa Conference, Leiden, The Netherlands, 1995.

Kaelan, *A short guide to the Lara Jonggrang temple group*, Jakarta: Jawatan Kedudayaan Departemen P. D. dan K, 1963.

Kavi, Ramakrishna., ed., *Bharatamuni's Nāṭyaśāstra*, vol. II, ed. Baroda: Gaekwad Oriental Series, LXVIII, 1934.

Khanna, V. and Saran, M., 'The Rāmāyaṇa Kakawin: a product of Sanskrit scholarship and independent literary genius', *Bijdragen tot de Taal-, Land en Volkenkunde*, 149, 2, 1993.

Klokke, M. J., *Tantri reliefs on ancient Javanese candi*, Leiden: KITLV Press, 1993.

Levin, C., 'The *Rāmāyaṇa, Rāmakatha* and *Loro Jonggrang*', Paper presented at the VIth International Conference of the European Association of Southeast Asian Archaeologists, Leiden, The Netherlands, 1996.

Nihom, M., 'Old Javanese *Rāmāyaṇa*', 25.25 and 24.117 ab: 'A Study in Literature and Pāśupata Śaivism', *Asiatische Studien /Etudes Asiatiques*, L3, 1996.

Richman, P., ed., *Many Rāmāyaṇas, The Diversity of a Narrative Tradition in South Asia*, Delhi: Oxford University Press, 1991.

Sedyawati, E., 'The dramatic principles of Javanese narrative temple reliefs' in B. Arps (ed), *Performance in Java and Bali. Studies of narrative, theatre, music and dance,* London: School of Oriental and African Studies, University of London, 1993.

Soedarsono, *Wayang Wong. The State Ritual Dance Drama in the Court of Yogyakarta,* Yogyakarta: Gadjah Mada University Press, 1984.

Soewito Santoso, *Rāmāyaṇa Kakawin,* 3 vols., Singapore/New Delhi: Institute of Southeast Asian Studies/International Academy of Indian Culture, 1980.

Stutterheim, W., *Rāma Legends and Rāma Reliefs in Indonesia,* New Delhi: Indira Gandhi National Centre for the Arts/ International Academy of Indian Culture, 1987.

Subarno, *Guide to the Prambanan temple,* Yogyakarta: Yogya ADV, 1991.

Vickers, A., *Bali. A Paradise Created,* Berkeley/Singapore: Periplus Editions, 1989.

Wallis, R.H., *The Voice as a Mode of Cultural Expression in Bali,* PhD dissertation, University of Michigan, 1980.

Zoetmulder, P.J., *Kalangawan,* The Hague: Martinus Nijhoff, 1974.

———, with the collaboration of S.O. Robson, *Old Javanese-English Dictionary,* 2 vols, 's-Gravenhage: Martinus Nijhoff, 1982.

3

The Framing of the Shrew

Kaikeyī as Kalahā in the Ānanda-Rāmāyaṇa

Vidyut Aklujkar

Abstract

THE account of Kalahā, the quarrelsome one, in *Ānanda-Rāmāyaṇa* (a fifteenth-century text in Sanskrit) appears in the context of the former birth of Kaikeyī, the stepmother of Rāma. Kaikeyī's demands bring about Prince Rāma's exile in the forest instead of his expected ascension to the throne, and alter the course of the epic irreversibly. In the present paper, I discuss in detail the account of Kalahā as an explanatory device for Kaikeyī's unmotherly behaviour. In particular, I compare it with similar accounts from the *Padma, Liṅga* and *Skanda* Purāṇas, and the epic *Mahābhārata*. This leads to a detailed discussion of the character of Kalahā, or the shrew, who is portrayed as an undesirable woman, or a woman too clever for her own good, or in general, a troublesome female. I connect the shrew with other portrayals of the troublesome female, such as Alakṣmī, Caṇḍī, Jyeṣṭhā or Avadasā. After taking a long detour of various characterisations of the shrew, I return to the *Ānanda Rāmāyaṇa* and its resolution of the question of Kaikeyī, in which Kaikeyī finally attains wisdom, and becomes one with *Brahman*.

Kaikeyī, the favourite queen of King Daśaratha of Ayodhyā, is instrumental in changing the entire course of action in

Vālmīki's *Rāmāyaṇa* (hereafter *VR*) from happy to tragic. King Daśaratha has given her two boons for her invaluable help to him on the battlefield. She can ask for whatever she wants but she has chosen to wait. When the King decides to consecrate the eldest prince, Rāma, as his successor, Kaikeyī demands that her own son, Bharata, be declared the crown prince, and Rāma sent to live in the forest for 14 years. Although her untimely demands alter the course of Rāma's life, Kaikeyī is given scant treatment in the original epic. In fact, in *VR*, there is a sharp line that divides Kaikeyī's life into pictures of 'before' and 'after'. Before these demands, she is the most beautiful, the most helpful, and the most beloved queen of Daśaratha, but after the unfortunate demands, she is subject only to censure, harsh words, anger and curses. The distraught King Daśaratha begs and cajoles her to change her mind, and when she does not budge, he utters indignant protests, and subjects her to harsh reprimands and curses.[1] Her co-wife, Rāma's mother Kauśalyā, calls her a rampant snake, a demoness and the killer of the entire clan.[2] Her stepson Lakṣmaṇa criticises her in venomous words, her daughter-in-law Sītā calls her discordant, the entire populace of Ayodhyā is angered by her selfish demands and wants to follow Rāma into the forest rather than live in the kingdom where she dwells, and finally, her own son Bharata, for whose sake she has secured the kingdom, curses her to hell,[3] and pierces her with the most pointed verbal arrows. He says the only reason he does not actually kill her is the fear of a chilling reprimand by his eldest brother Rāma.[4] Although she has robbed him of everything that was rightfully his, the only one who does not

1. *VR*, 2.7.33; 2.11. 5;
2. *VR*, 2.38.2
3. *VR*, 2.68.4; also 2.68.2, and 9.
4. *VR*, 2.72.21.

bear a grudge against Kaikeyī is Rāma himself. However, from this time onward, Kaikeyī fades into the background in *VR* and we do not hear about her much.

In subsequent retellings and reworkings of *Rāmāyaṇa*, poets have tried to make sense of Kaikeyī's actions. In the present paper, I shall examine the treatment of Kaikeyī in *Ānanda-Rāmāyaṇa*,[5] a fifteenth-century meta-*Rāmāyaṇa* in Sanskrit, and focus on the account of Kaikeyī's former life as a quarrelsome female, Kalahā. I shall discuss how such an account works to underscore Kaikeyī's selfish behaviour. In the course of my discussion, I shall compare the account of Kalahā with other accounts of the shrew in classical Indian literature. In the end, I shall argue that although *ĀR* amalgamates the most negative conceptions of female character into Kaikeyī/Kalahā, it breaks away from the irredeemable characterisation of Alakṣmī or Jyeṣṭhā by the various Purāṇas in that both Kalahā and Kaikeyī are finally transformed and redeemed in *ĀR*. This argument will be based on the analysis of several accounts of shrews or undesirable females, and also on the Kaikeyī-related incidents in *ĀR*, especially the last one where Kaikeyī finally achieves the knowledge of *Brahman* and attains salvation at the hands of Rāma. All the while, the original epic, *VR*, will serve as my background against which I shall discuss the *ĀR* innovations.

Vālmīki Rāmāyaṇa, being an epic, sets forth many model characters which excel in the virtue of selflessness. Each of these willingly sacrifices something worthwhile for the sake of others — for example, Rāma, the ideal son who leaves the kingdom for the sake of his father's word, Lakṣmaṇa, the ideal brother who leaves a wife and a life of luxury to

5. For more information on the dating of the *ĀR*, see Bulcke, 1971, p. 224. For discussion of various myths and humour of *ĀR*, see Vidyut Aklujkar, 1991, 1995, pp. 107-18, and also some forthcoming articles.

accompany Rāma into the forest, Sītā, the ideal wife who leaves the comforts of the palace to be with her husband, Kauśalyā and Sumitrā, the ideal mothers who wish the best for their sons, but still sacrifice their sons to the ideals of trustworthiness and family loyalty, Hanumān, the ideal helper/servant who puts his own life in danger to help the human prince and so on. Kaikeyī's character is at odds with the other mostly ideal characters of the epic, and hence, it is subjected to different treatments in the later retellings. She starts out as the youngest,[6] the most beautiful, and the most beloved wife of the king, and also his help-mate on the battleground. These are the qualities that win for her the two boons that Daśaratha promises her. But her one wrong action of demanding the two boons at the wrong time and in the wrong manner, results in horrendous consequences for everyone concerned. Kaikeyī turns into a cruel stepmother, an unwise mother to Bharata and a widow of Daśaratha who dies of a broken heart over his beloved son Rāma's exile. While reading this part (Ayodhyā Kāṇḍa) of *VR*, one witnesses how a generous queen who actually loves Rāma like her own son metamorphoses into a selfish, mean stepmother thanks to the evil counsels of her old nurse-maid, Mantharā. *VR* mentions Kaikeyī being very happy at the news that Rāma is going to be the crown prince. She rewards the news-bearing servant, Mantharā, with an ornament and speaks of her happiness as only natural, since everyone likes Rāma, and so this news is an occasion for great joy. Nevertheless, after she listens to the servant's slanderous

---

6. *ĀR* and the subsequent *Rāmāyaṇa* tradition in Mahārāṣṭra regard Kaikeyī as the youngest wife. *VR* refers to her as the middle mother [*madhyamāmbā*] and many scholars believe that she was the middle wife as well. But Prof. M.G. Dhadphale has argued that in *VR* she was the youngest wife but the middle mother, since she gave birth before Sumitrā. Since he has not yet published this hypothesis, I rely on his statement to that effect from a private correspondence with me.

fear-mongering, she changes her mind, and demands the two fateful boons. Kaikeyī's pivotal act of demanding two boons with immediate disastrous effects and her stubbornness in the face of Daśaratha's grief gives rise to many questions. Why does Kaikeyī do what she does? Does she not love Rāma? Has she no concern for her husband's well-being? Is she really a wicked wife, or is she only a jealous stepmother? Is she even a good mother? How can she not recognise her own son's mind? What is Kaikeyī's fault? Is it real selfishness, malice, or lack of judgement and shortsightedness. Who gets the ultimate blame for the tragic turn of events — Kaikeyī, or Mantharā who could overpower her mistress? Or is it the divine will or Destiny?[7]

It seems that in order to answer such questions, subsequent *Rāmāyaṇas* introduce alternate accounts which trace the causes of Kaikeyī's actions into the past and attempt to exculpate Kaikeyī somehow. The southern version of *VR*, for example, includes an account of Kaikeyī's mother who shows a fatal disregard for her husband's well-being, and insists on knowing why he laughed on an occasion even when he tells her that revealing the answer will result in his instant death. This is an attempt to place the blame of Kaikeyī's bad behaviour on her upbringing and on her mother's equally despicable behaviour.

In *VR*, Kaikeyī is decidedly the wicked wife, who has no regard for the sorrow of her husband, and with her actions brings about the death of Daśaratha. She is thereby placed against Sītā, who is regarded as one of the ideal wives in the Indian tradition. Sītā calls Kaikeyī *kalaha-śīlā*, the discordant one.[8]

ĀR, a fifteenth-century meta-*Rāmāyaṇa* and an influential compendium of myth and folklore, takes this cue from *VR*

---

7. Rāma attributes Kaikeyī's changed behaviour to Destiny. *VR*, 2.19.14.
8. *VR*, 6.23.4

and offers an amusing account of her past birth to highlight the character of Kaikeyī as the female who preferred *kalaha*, or discord. *ĀR* portrays Kaikeyī not just as a wicked wife, but also a mean mother and a malicious mother-in-law. To illustrate the last aspect of her character, a story, with the flavour of a folk narrative, relates how Kaikeyī is instrumental in sending Sītā to the forest the second time. In this account, Kaikeyī asks Sītā to describe Rāvaṇa. Sītā says that she never looked at his face; by keeping her gaze on the ground, she only saw his toes. Kaikeyī asks her to draw Rāvaṇa's big toe on a wall, Sītā complies in good faith and departs. Kaikeyī then completes the drawing herself and when Rāma comes by, she shows it to Rāma, insinuating that Sītā still contemplates Rāvaṇa. This is said to hasten Rāma's decision to abandon Sītā in the forest although she is pregnant.

Although *ĀR* includes many such tales to heighten the faults of selfishness and malice in Kaikeyī's character, its stand regarding the allotment of ultimate blame is ambiguous. On the one hand, it shows Kaikeyī as a selfish woman in this birth and the past birth, and seems to trace the vice of selfishness to the residue of her past life's *saṁskāras*, and on the other hand, it also attributes the ultimate blame for her actions to the desire of the Gods that Rāvaṇa, the Demon King, should be vanquished and killed at the hands of Rāma. All the actions of all the characters in this meta-*Rāmāyaṇa* are ultimately destined to happen by the divine will of Rāma who is understood there as essentially Viṣṇu and ultimately as the cosmic reality, *Brahman*. On that level of ultimate realisation, whatever happens is only the *līlā*, or play, of the cosmic reality. But that does not preclude anyone from attributing mundane motives and blame to people in their daily lives.

Unlike *VR*, *ĀR* does not forget Kaikeyī. *ĀR* narrates how at the end Kaikeyī overcomes her main vice of selfishness and becomes a better person. It does this in the most innovative fashion. The Kaikeyī of *ĀR* is a multi-faceted, human character, and she has been given the final instruction into the knowledge of *Brahman* by the compassionate Rāma. I shall save the end of Kaikeyī till the end of this paper, and start before the beginning — that is, with the former life of Kaikeyī as Kalahā which is described at great length in the Sārakāṇḍa 4.117-5.41. Here I offer excerpts from my translations.[9]

> King Daśaratha asked the sage Mudgala, "Who was I in my former life, and what good deeds did I do, that Hari became my son Rāmacandra, and Lakṣmī herself became my daughter-in-law Sītā? Please tell me all about it, O Brahmin."
>
> Mudgala said, "In the vicinity of Sahyādri, long ago, in the Karavīra city, there was a Brahmin named Dharmadatta, who was knowledgeable about religion, and used to be immersed always in the worship of Viṣṇu and in observing ritual vows before Viṣṇu. He was well-versed in the 12-letter *mantra* (*auṁ namo bhagavate vāsudevāya*), fond of chanting, and hospitable. Once in the month of Kārttika, he took the utensils of

9. There is no complete translation into English of the text. I have provided partial translations as needed in articles written on the text. My complete translation and an edition of the text in progress, are based on (1) an early printed edition published from Bombay, by Govardhandas Lakhmidas, in *pothī* form with no date of publication and some pages of earlier chapters missing, (2) a Marāṭhī translation by Pandit Vishnushastri Bapat published by Dā. Sāṁ. Yande, in 1900, [I have secured two pages of the *'prastāvanā'* or preface to this edition, but not the translation], and (3) a Hindi commentary called *Jyotsnā* written by Pandit Rāmtej Pandey and included in *ĀR* published by Pandit Yugal Kishor Dwivedi, Varanasi: Pandit Pustakālaya, 1977. Also see Aruna Gupta, *Ānanda-Rāmāyaṇa: A Cultural Study*, Dehli: Eastern Book Linkers, 1984.

worship and went to the temple of Hari in the last quarter of the night in order to chant Hari's name and keep awake. That is when he noticed a fiend (*kṛtyā*) making horrible noise and approaching him. She had crooked fangs, lolling tongue, red eyes, dried up flesh, and drooping lips. She was stark naked, dressed in space alone, and she was making a terrible uproar. As he saw her, the priest was overcome with fright, and began to shake all over. He uttered the name of Hari, and threw at her the utensils of worship and milk from his hands. Since she was hit by the water with *tulasī* leaves, along with the name of Hari, the effect of her sins wore off, and she began to remember her former birth, and started to bow down and speak about it.

The fiend said, 'Due to the effect of my former deeds, I have come to this state of affairs. Now tell me, priest, how can I attain to the best state?'

Dharmadatta said, 'Tell me everything in detail: by which deeds did you attain this state, where do you come from, and what was your character?'

The fiend said, 'There was a Brahmin named Bhikṣu in a city in Saurāṣṭra. O priest, I was his wife, known as Kalahā (the quarrelsome one) and extremely callous. Even if my husband begged me, I never did anything to please him. I always went against his wishes, or his speech, and never gave him good food to eat. At the time of cooking I would eat first whatever good was there, and then only pass it on to my husband. Once my husband told his friend all about me. He said, "My wife does not listen to my words at all! What should I do?" The friend listened to it all, thought for a moment, and said to my husband, "I will tell you a trick. Tell your wife to do the opposite of what you want done. Thus when you use the negative mode of speech, she will accomplish whatever you want." My husband followed the advice of the friend and came home and told me, "My dear, never invite my friend to dinner. He is the biggest scoundrel." When I heard his words, I told him, "Your friend is the best Brahmin, and the other sages praise him. I will certainly invite him for dinner today." Saying so, I went and invited that friend of my husband's. Since then, my husband started to deal with me by telling me not to do what he wanted done. Once when the date of his father's death anniversary (*śrāddha*) approached, he said to me, "My dear, I will not observe the ritual of *śrāddha* for my father." As I heard that speech of my husband's, I scolded him, saying, "*Dhik, Dhik!* How will you not observe the *śrāddha* ! Don't you know the duty of a son? What state will you attain to!" So he told me, "Then don't cook any sweets today. Invite only one Brahmin, do not extend the invitation to more." When I heard that, I invited eighteen Brahmins, the Gods on earth, and made all kinds of sweets for the ritual meal. Then again he said to me, "My beloved, listen to what I say. First eat with me all the meal, and then serve our own leftovers to the priests." So I scolded my husband again, "How can you eat first and then serve the guests?" Thus he made me do the whole *śrāddha* ritual by talking to me in negation. When he finished the offering of *piṇḍa*s, he said to me, "It seems that I will fast today." But of course, then I made him eat all the sweets. Then somehow he forgot himself, and instructed me to take the *piṇḍa*s and deposit them in some holy waters. At that, I took those and dumped them into a cesspool. My husband was stunned to see that, and miserable at heart, he began to wail. He thought for a minute, and said, "Don't you take the *piṇḍa*s out again." So I got down into the pit and rescued them. Then he said, "Don't ever throw them into holy waters," so I went and with great respect, deposited them into the *Tīrtha* waters. Thus, I was so fond of quarreling that I never once did what my husband wanted. As he became totally disenchanted with me and began contemplating another wife, I took poison and committed suicide. Then the attendants of Yama (God of Death) tied me up and took me to him. Yama glanced at me and asked the scribe Citragupta, "What good or bad deeds has this one performed? Citragupta, find out her balance sheet, and tell me what rewards is she going to get?"

Citragupta then looked at me and said censuring me, "She has not done any good deed at all. She ate sweetmeats herself, but did not offer them to her husband. Therefore she should go to the birth of a crane, and will live eating her own excrement. She always hated her husband, and always quarreled. Therefore, she should live the excrement-eating dog's life. She used to eat stealthily whatever she saved in the cooking pot. Therefore she should become a cat, who eats her own young. She also committed suicide in order to hurt her husband, so she should suffer in the form of a fiend as well. She is especially hateful, and should be carried away by your attendants to a deserted place, where she should be made to endure being a fiend, and then she should endure the three other births as well."

Kalahā the fiend continued, "While wandering about in the shape of a fiend, I attacked you. Due to the contact of the water mixed with *tulasī* leaves, I washed away all my sins. Now, O King of Brahmins, do me a favour and please free me from the three future births as well. O Great sage, I am at your feet, please release me from those three, and from this fiend-like existence."

Having heard this speech of Kalahā, the Brahmin became full of sorrow due to realising the misery of her former life's actions. He witnessed her suffering and was moved by pity. He meditated for a while and spoke with great sorrow the following good words. [*ĀR Sarga* 5]

"May you obtain good goals by the half of my entire life's savings of merit points generated by my *Kārttika vrata*. It is certain that all holy waters, sacrificial oblations and holy observances will not be equivalent to the merits acquired by the observance of *Kārttika vrata*."

Mudgala said, "Having spoken thus, Dharmadatta sprinkled on her the holy waters mixed with *tulasī*, and let her hear the *mantra* of twelve syllables. Right away she was freed of the fiendish state, and she became as beautiful as Urvaśī, splendid as the burning flame of a lamp, with a divine body. Then she fell to the ground like a stick, bowed at the Brahmin's feet, and said to him the following words in a voice choked with happiness."

Kalahā said, "O best of brāhmaṇas, thanks to your mercy, I am freed from hell. You have indeed been a boat to me as I was sinking in the sea of sins."

While speaking thus, she noticed an aeroplane descending from the skies, and divine troops resembling Viṣṇu were sitting in it.

[*The troops praise the brāhmaṇa for his generosity and his religious behaviour, and promise a lengthy stay in heaven enjoying all pleasures. They speak further.*]

"From heaven, when you exhaust your merit, you will descend to the face of the earth, and will become a famous king in the Sun dynasty, called Daśaratha, and will have two wives. There is no doubt that this Kalahā who shared the half of your life's merit will become your third wife, Kaikeyī. Even there, on the earth, Viṣṇu will keep your company and become your son, called Rāma. In order to perform his divine duty, he will kill the demons such as Rāvaṇa, and will rule the world."

Mudgala said, "Having instructed Dharmadatta thus, they sat with him and Kalahā in the plane and went to Vaikuṇṭha heaven. Dharmadatta too, with his yearly observance of the vrata, attained the desirable state along with his wives at the end of his bodily existence. Having lived in the Vaikuṇṭha abode for many thousands of years, when he exhausted his merit, he was born as a great king with three wives. O king Daśaratha, God Viṣṇu took birth as your son Rāma, and Śeṣa became Lakṣmaṇa, Brahmā became Bharata, and the Wheel became Śatrughna.

> Thus have I narrated everything, since you asked for it. Blessed are you whose son is the very Nārāyaṇa."

ĀR in the above account supplies a framework of a former life of Kalahā, the shrew, to the character of Kaikeyī. Let us analyse what narrative functions are served by the inclusion of this account. There is no question of the entertainment value of such an account. One can also imagine the local colour and detailed embellishments that can be added to such an account by a priest who reads it at a temple to a gathering of listeners and comments on it at the *kathā-purāṇa* session. Apart from these, the immediate use of such an account in the course of the epic narration is in linking the characterisation of Kaikeyī to the vice of selfishness in more ways than one. The line of reasoning seems to be as follows. A woman is a wife before she becomes a mother. If she is mean as a mother, it is likely that she was wicked as a wife as well. Kaikeyī's main action in *VR* portrays her as a mean stepmother to Rāma and an unwise mother to Bharata. However, before that instant, she is actually the best-loved and most helpful wife of Daśaratha. *ĀR* carries over her characterisation as a mean mother, but in order to underscore her role as a wicked wife, it shows her in a former life also as a wicked wife. In her life as Kalahā, there is no mention of children, and still the woman is self-centered and has no regard for the well-being of her husband. Her faults are compounded and severely punished in four horrible future births. She is also shown as shortsighted because she thinks only of getting what she wants right now without thinking of the long-term consequences of her actions. These faults of hers can be seen as links between the narration of Kalahā and the next narration of Kaikeyī. By framing Kaikeyī as Kalahā, *ĀR* seems to draw parallels to demonstrate how Kaikeyī was overcome with momentary selfishness and without pondering the long-term consequences of her demands on the king, the princes and the kingdom, insisted on fulfilling her two boons at all costs.

Leaving Kaikeyī aside for a while, I would like to concentrate on the character of Kalahā, the quarrelsome female, who later on is born as Kaikeyī. I would like to compare the portrayal of Kalahā to similar accounts of other undesirable females. In this analysis I would like to show how *ĀR* combines two distinct characters of ancient times in one to create a remarkable caricature of an undesirable female such as Kalahā. Her character shows the flip side of the concept of the ideal female in Sanskrit literature. For some time I have been engaged in researching the concept of an ideal female and have written papers on ideal wives (*pativratās*) such as Anasūyā,[10] Lopāmudrā,[11] Sāvitrī,[12] and others. This study in the conception of the antithesis of an ideal woman is complementary to my former studies and serves to offer a balanced picture of the female in the Indian psyche.

When I started to search other parallel accounts of a quarrelsome female, I found that the account in *Padma Purāṇa,* Uttarakhaṇda, (*adhyāya* 106-7) was the origin of much of the Kalahā account of *ĀR.* In fact, I found out that they are similar in verses with very minor verbal differences, except that the *Padma Purāṇa* account is very brief about the actual behaviour of Kalahā. It simply says,

> In a city in Saurāṣṭra lived a brāhmaṇa named Bhikṣu, and I was his very cruel wife, named Kalahā. Never did I do anything good for my husband, not even in words. I did not give him any sweet food, I loved to quarrel and always did the opposite of what he said.

10. See Aklujkar, in Bose, 2000, pp. 56-68.
11. See Aklujkar, in Richman, 2001.
12. See Aklujkar, in Sharma, 1991, pp. 324-33.

> So my husband was scared and disgusted and began to think of taking another wife. Thereafter I took poison and gave up my life, O brāhmaṇa.

To this bland account of a quarrelsome wife, *ĀR* has added the account of Kalahā's actual behaviour, the frustration of her husband, his confiding it to his friend, the solution offered by the friend, the practice of reverse psychology by Kalahā's husband on her, his limited success, the incident of his father's *śrāddha*, and the final anti-climax when he forgets himself for a brief moment, and lapses into the normal mode of speech with disastrous consequences. *ĀR*'s addition of all these details certainly makes the account of Kalahā more entertaining.

I would have given the credit for this entertaining account to *ĀR* had I not been troubled by a faint memory of one just such wife, about whom our mothers and teachers always warned us. This troublesome female was always there as a negative norm in my childhood, a woman whom you should never imitate. She was sometimes called Caṇḍī, and sometimes Avadasā, but always remembered as the wife of sage Uddālaka. Any spirited woman, if she was judged to be too independent for her own good, was compared to sage Uddālaka's wife.[13] She would always do the opposite of what her husband wanted. This proverbial wife has a lot in common with the remainder of our *ĀR* account of Kalahā.

Further search landed me onto an account of Caṇḍī, the wife of sage Uddālaka, from a Marāṭhī children's book,

---

13. Uddālaka ṛṣīcī bāyako [Wife of Sage Uddālaka] is the title of a short story by Gaurī Deshpande, a contemporary feminist author. In it she describes a woman who marries a man for no other reason than to spite her mother, just because her mother forbids her to marry him.

Babhruvāhana, by Pandit Mahadev Shastri Joshi.[14] Her story is very similar to our Kalahā's story, especially the account of her father-in-law's *śrāddha*, but there, the frame-story is different. The context is of Arjuna moving along with Yudhiṣṭhira's sacrificial horse, when the horse gets stuck to a boulder in the Vindhya mountains, and no amount of force can get the horse unstuck. Inquiries by Arjuna lead him to hear an account of an unfortunate female, Caṇḍī, the wife of sage Uddālaka, who always did the opposite of what her husband wanted. The entire story of her contrary behaviour, her husband's frustrations, his friend's advice, the husband practising reverse psychology on his wife, the partial success, the incident of his father's death anniversary rituals, and the final disaster due to the sage's slip into the normal mode of speech, all these details are there. But the story is different at that point. The angered sage curses his contrary wife, and petrifies her just as Ahalyā was petrified earlier by her angered husband, sage Gautama, in post-*VR Rāmāyaṇas*. Sage Uddālaka says to his wife,

> You will become a boulder and live a life of an obstacle. When Arjuna comes with the sacrificial horse that horse will get stuck to you, and will be obstructed. When Arjuna's hand touches the boulder, you will be redeemed, and your curse will end.

The wife of Uddālaka is the contrary wife in older accounts, and is most likely the source of the other half of the Kalahā account of *ĀR*. This clever grafting of two quarrelsome females into one has some poetic merits. Besides being dramatic and

14. The *Bhāratavarṣīya Prācīna Caritra Kośa* notes that the source of Caṇḍī, the wife of Uddālaka, whose story is like Kalahā's story, is Jaiminīya Aśvamedha 16. The story appears in a summary translation in the introduction of the *Mahābhārata*, Aśvamedha Parvan, vol. 16, tr. R.D. Karmarkar, ed. V.S. Sukathankar, S.D. Belvalkar.

humorous, it incorporates motifs such as an insufferable wife, a wife who is an obstacle[15] (literally or figuratively) in the path of sacrifice, a wife who has utter disregard for the husband's ancestors (Caṇḍī and Kalahā), or his entire clan (Kaikeyī), and a wife who will suffer for many births unless redeemed by a touch of divinity. (Arjuna's touch transforms the boulder into the sage's wife, whereas the touch of the holy water from the brāhmaṇa's worship transforms Kalahā into a virtuous beauty.) One may also realise that inside every shrew or cursed female is a desirable woman waiting to come out. It only takes a Petruchio to woo the wild cat, or a Dharmadatta to sprinkle the blessed water on the fiend and share half his lifetime's merit to redeem her.

We saw the account of the contrary behaviour of sage Uddālaka's wife from Jaimini-*aśvamedha*, which is grafted by *ĀR* onto Kalahā's story. Further search reveals that Uddālaka's wife is none other than Alakṣmī'[16] or Jyeṣṭhā in Purāṇic accounts. These two names and corresponding characterisations are found in some older Purāṇic accounts of the churning of the ocean by Gods and Demons to obtain the nectar of immortality. The *Padma Purāṇa* Brahmakhaṇḍa, *adhyāya*s 9-10 relate that as the gods and demons went on churning, first emerged the Kālakūṭa poison, and right after that came out Alakṣmī, an utterly undesirable female, the opposite of Lakṣmī or prosperity. Besides being the epitome of horrible appearance,[17] she also was the most unfortunate female, who

15. The motif of a wife as a boulder, or literally an obstacle in the path of the husband's well-being is not limited to the realm of myths such as Ahalyā and Caṇḍī, but has become proverbial in Marāṭhī. The contrary wife is called *'mārgātīl dhoṇḍ'* meaning 'a boulder in the path'.

16. *Liṅga Purāṇa* Uttara, 2. 6 *Alakṣmī-varṇanam nāma ṣaṣṭhodhyāyam* ।

17. In classical Sanskrit literature, physical beauty and virtuousness often go hand in hand. Inversely, ugliness of appearance is associated with vice, and sometimes these traits are traced to meritorious or otherwise deeds done in past births.

was sent by Gods to dwell only wherever there are discord, discontent, and dysfunctional families. The appearance of Alakṣmī from the ocean was followed by that of Lakṣmī, the most beautiful divine damsel, who is prosperity or Śrī incarnate. Now Viṣṇu wanted to marry her, but Lakṣmī said, "Without marrying off the Eldest One [literally Jyeṣṭhā], My Lord, how will you marry me, the younger one?"[18] At that, Viṣṇu gave away the elder sister in marriage to sage Uddālaka, and took the younger one, Lakṣmī as his own consort. At this point, the account of Alakṣmī and Uddālaka ends abruptly, but is taken up again several chapters later, in the Uttarakhaṇḍa of *Padma Purāṇa* in *adhyāya* 116 *(alakṣmī-vṛttānta-varṇanam)* Here, the impossibility of such a match becomes obvious. Uddālaka wants to take his newly-wed wife to an *āśrama* where there are sacrifices and holy chanting of the Vedic *mantras*, and she says,

> Sorry, I cannot dwell here. I cannot live in a place where there are sacrifices, Vedic chants and worship of ancestors and guests. I can only dwell where the brāhmaṇas are insulted, where the cows are slaughtered, where there are falsehood, quarrels, excessive drinking, debauchery, and dysfunctionality.

When he hears this, poor sage Uddālaka panics. He tells her to stay under an *aśvattha* tree while he goes to find a suitable place for her, and promptly deserts her. She begins to wail when she realises this. Lakṣmī hears her wails in heaven and implores Viṣṇu, 'My elder sister is crying because her husband

18. Echoes of this will be found in Baptista's declaration 'Gentlemen, importune me no farther. For how I firmly am resolved, you know, That is, not to bestow my younger daughter, before I have a husband for the elder.' Shakespeare, Taming of the Shrew, Act 1, scene 1. This is not so much an indication of actual borrowing, but suggests common understanding of parental responsibility.

has deserted her. We should help her.' So Viṣṇu goes to Alakṣmī and tells her to dwell under the *aśvattha* tree, and promises that her sister Lakṣmī will come to visit her every Saturday. After that she dwells there, and also frequents the places of discord where she likes to visit.

This account of Alakṣmī[19] portrays her in the most extreme colours. By her very nature, and by the divine will, she is totally irreconcilable. The only way to deal with a wife who is so opposed to righteousness seems to be to leave her. Some overtones of Uddālaka's desertion of his despicable wife can be heard in the *VR* narration when Daśaratha verbally discards Kaikeyī by forbidding her to touch him at his last hour. He says,

> Kaikeyī, do not touch me. I do not wish to see you. You are not my wife, nor a relation to me. Since you are bent upon achieving your goal at any cost (*kevalārtha-parāṁ*), without regard to righteous conduct (*tyakta-dharmāṁ*), I am deserting you. (*tyajāmy aham*).[20]

Since in *VR*, Sitā is an incarnation of Lakṣmī, and since Kaikeyī is posited as the antithesis of Sitā in wifely virtues, it is likely that some resonances of the ancient concept of Alakṣmī may have appeared in the *VR* portrayal of Kaikeyī. Besides the verbal desertion by Daśaratha, Kaikeyī gets mostly a silent treatment in *VR* in that she lives in Ayodhyā, and goes places along with the other widows, but we hardly ever hear anything from her in the later cantos of *VR*.

ĀR, on the other hand, does not give Kaikeyī the silent treatment of most of the *VR*. It delineates the past, the present

---

19. Also other such accounts from *Liṅga Purāṇa* II, 6 and 76 [*alakṣmī-vāsa-yogya-sthānāni*].
20. *VR*, 2.37.7.

and also the future of the character of Kaikeyī. We saw how it generates the Kalahā-Kaikeyī equation to frame her in her past. We also noted how it avoids making Kaikeyī similar to the more extreme Alakṣmī accounts of the Purāṇas. In other words, *ĀR* follows only the milder, more humorous characterisations of Uddālaka's wife to frame Kaikeyī into a selfish, foolish wife in her former life as Kalahā, and also ensures that she is transformed, and revived by a kind husband, the brāhmaṇa Dharmadatta. This kind treatment of the fearsome female in the Kalahā story foreshadows the kinder treatment that Kaikeyī gets in the later portions of *ĀR* The brāhmaṇa Dharmadatta in the story of Kalahā is a virtuous, religious, and above all generous human being who is willing to offer half his lifetime's merit to save an unfortunate female from her miserable life. The suggestion seems to be that following Dharmadatta, Daśaratha in the next birth is also a gallant soul, who is generous in giving away his life's most precious possessions like Rāma to satisfy others. Thus, the account of Dharmadatta saving Kalahā in *ĀR* seems to render a psychologically complex past-birth context to the later account of Daśaratha and Kaikeyī.

Now we come to the end of the Kalahā/Kaikeyī narration. Kalahā is revived by her future husband. However, it is impossible for Kaikeyī to be redeemed by her husband since he dies as a result of her actions. Rāma, the supreme lord comes to her rescue instead. In the penultimate book of *ĀR* (*Manoharakāṇḍa* 2.52-101) Kaikeyī approaches Rāma with humility and apologises for her past misconduct, which she blames on her ignorance, and actually entreats him to forgive her. Rāma replies 'You are not guilty of your former actions against me. It was by my command that Sarasvatī the Goddess of Speech appeared in your mouth and uttered the demands of the two boons. Therefore, you are pure, Kaikeyī. I am not angry at you.' Kaikeyī requests Rāma to instruct and enlighten her. Rāma replies that Lakṣmaṇa will take her for an outing the next morning and will give her the necessary instruction.

The next day he tells Lakṣmaṇa to take Kaikeyī in a palanquin to a field where there are many sheep and let her see and hear the sheep. Lakṣmaṇa does as he is told. Kaikeyī is suspicious at first and while looking at the field full of sheep she wonders why Rāma has sent her there, and whether he intends to make fun of her. However, as she begins to hear the noise of the sheep, 'Me, me, me', she begins to think. 'Why are all these sheep saying 'me, me, me', she wonders.' In an instant, it dawns on her that she and everyone else are like those sheep, always saying 'Me, me, me', or 'mine, mine, mine' and deluded by the possessive tendency called *mamatā*. She tells Lakṣmaṇa that she has fulfilled the purpose of her excursion, and he takes her back to Rāma. She informs Rāma that she understood the message of the sheep and will teach it also to others. The message is that all throughout our life, in this birth and in all other births, we are deluded because we hold on to things and people as 'mine', and of course, that leads to divisions, jealousies, and misery. When we realise that our attitude of mineness (*me-me-vṛtti* or *mamatā*) is just a delusion, then we can realise the futility of it all, and are ready to be one with the cosmic reality, *Brahman*. Rāma says to her, 'Right you are, Kaikeyī, you interpreted the speech of the sheep in the right manner. Now go ahead and live in peace. You are a *jīvan-mukta*, a living-liberated soul.'

In the proper Indian tradition of not ending a story on a tragic note, *ĀR* has supplied this innovative ending to the character of Kaikeyī. Note that it resolves the ethical or moral question of guilt and blame also by the characteristic Indian manner of gaining enlightenment, rather than by repentance, or punishment alone. Living a life of lonely widowhood and alienation from her co-wives and her son is punishment indeed for Kaikeyī. *ĀR* creates Kalahā to frame Kaikeyī into a mould of a wicked wife, albeit with a possibility of redemption and on the metaphysical level, it resolves the question of her blame and guilt by bringing in the divine will. Finally, instead of Rāma directly giving her instruction, letting the sheep serve as her metaphysical masters also adds a special dramatic and poetic flavour to the narration. It brings the beastly and the beatific together to redeem humanity. This is what Kaikeyī realises in the end:

> By the message in their speech and by your Grace, O Rāghava, the attitude of *'me me'*, mine, mine, is gone from me. I stand now here as liberated. When I had falsely understood this body as mine then I was attached to this world. Then what would I get in this world full of grief? Let my body be or let it get dissolved like a ripple on water. Who is the son? Who is a brother to whom? All this is *Brahman*, there is no doubt about it.

Table 1: Kalahā and Kaikeyī

Kalahā	*Kaikeyī*
• wife of a brāhmaṇa	• queen of King Daśaratha
• quarrelsome, contrary	• split between good/bad
• no regard for husband	• no regard for husband
• many wrong actions	• one wrong action
• on the blacklist of Citragupta	• on everyone's black list (except Rāma)
• punished in four horrible births	• punished in this very birth
• redeemed by Dharmadatta, later re-born as her husband Daśaratha	• Daśaratha dies because of her, but Rāma redeems her

Table 2: Connections

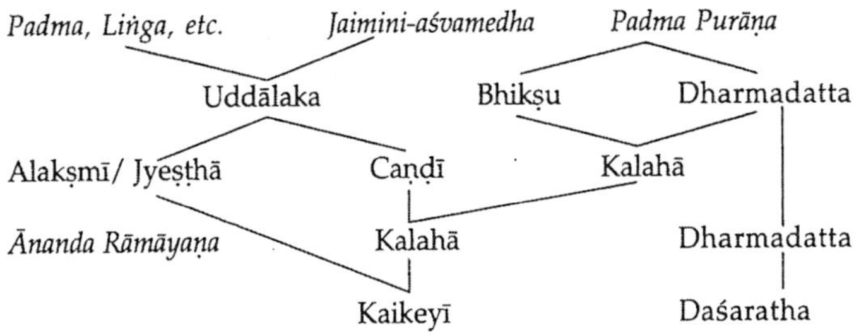

Bibliography

Aklujkar, V., 'Battle as Banquet : A Metaphor in Sūradāsa', *Journal of the American Oriental Society*, 111: 2, April-June, 1991.

———, 'Sāvitrī: Old and New', in Arvind Sharma (ed.), *Essays on the Mahābhārata*, Leiden: E. J. Brill, 1991.

———, 'Rāmāvatāra Recycled', *Annals of the Bhandarkar Oriental Research Institute*, vol. LXXVI, Pune: Bhandarkar Oriental Research Institute, 1995, pp.107-18.

———, 'Why Build A Bridge Over The Ocean: Propriety in The Ānanda Rāmāyaṇa', Paper presented at the Annual South Asia Conference, Madison, Wisconsin, 17 Oct. 1997, Forthcoming.

———, 'Crying Dogs and Laughing Trees in Rāma's Kingdom: Self- reflexivity in *Ānanda Rāmāyaṇa*', Paper presented at the Annual South Asia Conference, Madison, Wisconsin, 1998, Forthcoming.

———, 'Anasūyā : A Pativratā with Panache' in Mandakranta Bose (ed.), *Faces of the Feminine in Ancient Medieval and Modern India*, Oxford: Oxford University Press, 2000.

Altekar, G. S., *Studies on Vālmīki's Rāmāyaṇa*, Poona: Bhandarkar Oriental Research Institute, 1987.

Bose, Mandakranta (ed.), *Faces of the Feminine in Ancient Medieval and Modern India*, Oxford: Oxford University Press, 2000.

Brockington, J.L., *Righteous Rāma : The Evolution of an Epic*, Delhi: Oxford University Press, 1984.

Bulcke, Camille, *Rām-kathā: utpatti aur Vikās*, rev. edn., Allahabad: Allahabad University, 1971.

Chitrao, M. M., Siddheshwar Shastri, *Bhāratīya Prācina Caritrakośa* [Dictionary of Ancient Indian Biography in Hindi], Pune: Bhāratīya Charitrakośa Maṇḍaḷ, 1964.

Dvivedi, Pandit Yugalkishor (ed.), *Ānanda-Rāmāyaṇam* [With the commentary

'Jyotsnā' by Pandeya Ramtej Shastri], Vārāṇasī: Pandita Pustakalaya, 1977.

Goldman, Robert, P. (ed.) *The Rāmāyaṇa of Vālmīki : An Epic of Ancient India*, vol. 1- 5, Princeton, New Jersey: Princeton University Press, 1986.

Gorresia, Gasparo (ed.), *The Vālmīki Rāmāyaṇa* [North-eastern Recension], Madras: Indian Heritage Trust, 1981-82.

Gupta, Aruna, *Ānanda-Rāmāyaṇa: A Cultural Study*, Dehli: Eastern Book Linkers, 1984.

Krishnacharya, T.R. (ed.), *The Vālmīki Rāmāyaṇa* [Southern Recension] Delhi: Sri Satguru Publications, 1982.

Shah, Umakant Premchand (ed.), *The Vālmīki-Rāmāyaṇa*, Critical Edition, vols. 1-6, Baroda: Oriental Institute, 1960-75.

Sharma, Arvind (ed.), *Essays on the Mahābhārata*, Leiden: E. J. Brill, 1991.

Shastri, Jagadish (ed.), *Liṅgapurāṇam: A Stydy*, Delhi: Motilal Banarsidass, 1980.

Shastri Panasikar, Waudev Laxman (ed.), *The Rāmāyaṇa of Vālmīki* [Commentary Tilaka by Rāma], Delhi: Indological Book House, 1983.

Śrīmad Vālmīki Rāmāyaṇaṁ Śrīmad govindarājīya-rāmānujīya-taniślokī-māheśvaratīrthīyākhyā-vyākhyā-catuṣṭaya-samanvitaṁ, Bombay: Lakshmi Venkateshwar Press, 1935.

Thiel-Horstmann, Monika (ed.), *Rāmāyaṇa and Rāmāyaṇas*, vol. 3 in Barz and Thiel-Horstmann (eds.), *Khoj: A Series of Modern South Asian Studies*, Wiesbaden: Otto Harrassowitz, 1991.

Vālmīki Rāmāyaṇam: Text as Constituted in its Critical Edition, Baroda: Oriental Institute, 1992.

Vālmīkiya Rāmāyaṇaṁ [Hindi Translation] Gorakhpur: Gītā Press, 1990.

Vyāsa, Kṛṣṇa Dvaipāyana, *Padmapurāṇam. Ṣaṣṭham Uttarakhaṇḍam, pūrvārddham, caturtho bhāga*, Guru Mandala Granthamālā, vol. 18, 1959.

4

Three Ways of Falling in Love
Tulsīdās's Phulvārī Episode and the Way it is Portrayed in Contemporary Electronic Media

Heidi Pauwels

Abstract

ONE of the discrepancies of Tulsīdās's *Rāmcaritmānas,* compared to the Sanskrit *Rāmāyaṇa* attributed to Vālmīkī, is the addition of the Phulvārī episode, a romantic scene where Rāma and Sītā meet each other for the first time and fall in love. Tulsīdās had his own agenda for dwelling upon this scene, which was related to his *bhakti* message. The episode has been popular ever since, but its relevance seems to go beyond the *bhakti* message. Contemporary electronic versions of Sītā and Rāmā's 'premarital' love operate within a context where the pros and cons of love-marriages and arranged marriages are hotly debated. In this paper, I will compare the episode in Tulsī's *Rāmcaritmānas* with the TV version by Ramanand Sagar, so as to identify how the medieval message has been adapted for a contemporary public. In addition, by analysing a popular contemporary hit-movie, I will show how the new message spills over in the domain of popular culture for commercial consumption.

Introduction

In this paper, I will be concerned with a textual-comparative way of analysing the impact of the *Rāmāyaṇa* on contemporary public life, in particular gender relations, in South Asia. I will concentrate on how the relation between Rāma and Sītā functions as a model, in particular, how the way their courtship is portrayed sends messages to young people as regards the establishing of matrimonial relationships. I will do so by means of a case-study of one episode, and compare how this functions in three different texts.

The episode is the romantic scene where Rāma and Sītā meet each other for the first time before their marriage and fall in love. Interestingly, this episode does not occur in the 'Ur-text', the Sanskrit *Rāmāyaṇa* attributed to Vālmīki. However, that does not impede it from being an extremely popular one in the contemporary imagination [Lutgendorf 1991a: 94 (in *jhāṅkī* or tableau), 105 (in Kajli singing), 332 (in *Rāmlīlā* play); also 1994: 218]. In most versions, the episode is cast in the romantic settings of a flower garden, hence this scene is commonly referred to as the *puṣpa-vāṭikā* or *phulvārī* episode. Here, Rāma and Sītā meet by chance, while she is on her way to a nearby temple, and he is picking flowers for his guru's *pūjā*.

The three texts I have selected for this paper are two explicit retellings of the *Rāmāyaṇa* and one contemporary commercial movie that implicitly draws upon the story. One of the *Rāmāyaṇa* retellings is medieval in origin, but has gained in popularity over the centuries, and is arguably the most popular version today, namely Tulsīdās' *Rāmcaritmānas*. The other text is the TV version directed by Ramanand Sagar (Ramchand Chopra), which dates from the late eighties. It was first shown with immediate immense success on the official channel Durdarshan from 25 January 1987 till 31 July 1988, and its video version (pirated or legitimate) is still one of the items stocked in many 'Indian' grocery stores even in the U.S.

The third text I will take into account is a recent, extremely successful and trend-setting Bollywood movie. I have in mind the popular 1994 hit-movie *Hum aapke hain kaun,* 'What am I to you?' directed by Sooraj R. Barjatya. This movie is about family and marriage and concentrates mainly — to say it dryly — on the love story of a thwarted pair who seek to have their love sanctified as an 'arranged marriage'. Though not explicitly portraying the love of Rāma and Sītā, the movie heavily draws upon *Rāmāyaṇa* mythological images, as I will explain below.

The method used for this paper is textual: a comparative study of the 'first love' episode in different texts. Let me briefly explain the rationale for using this method.

If we want to understand what message the *Rāmāyaṇa* carries for contemporary South Asians, it makes sense to start with decoding the most successful modern electronic media form of the message and showing its complexity. Or, in the jargon, if the contemporary Indian spectator of movies is 'caught in an interocular field', and 'each site or setting for the socialising and regulation of the public gaze is to some degree affected by the experiences of the other sites', this paper aims at unravelling at least one thread of such 'substantive transfer of meaning' and 'interweaving of ocular experiences' (Breckenridge 1995). Simply put, if we want to investigate what the contemporary texts have to say, we need to lay our finger on how exactly the contemporary message makes use of and differs from the earlier ones.

I come from the discipline of textual studies, which means I will bracket for the purpose of this paper the audience reaction. I do not mean to imply that it would not be interesting and worthwhile to pursue reactions to the texts presented here. To the contrary, I hope this paper will inspire such a research project for someone in popular culture studies or anthropology. In particular, this is possible for the contemporary electronic texts. One could on the one hand interview the directors, on the other consult popular film magazines, reader's letters to newspapers and magazines or actually interview spectators to form an idea of the public's reception of those texts (keeping in mind the specifics of the interview situation; see Raheja 1994, 72-73). This is, however, a project outside the scope of this paper and my discipline. For our purpose, it may be sufficient to keep in mind that contemporary electronic versions of Sītā and Rāma's premarital love operate within a context where the pros and cons of 'love-marriages' and 'arranged marriages' are hotly debated (see, for instance, Derné 1995a: 122-40).

In any case, I see it as a logical first step to investigate the changes in 'the message' from a textual perspective, before we can understand the reactions of contemporary South Asians to these texts.

To provide an overview of how the message evolved over time, I will present the different versions of the episodes in chronological sequence. That is, I will start with highlighting the relevant features of Tulsīdās's episode. Then I will analyse Ramanand Sagar's TV version, so as to identify how the medieval message has been adapted for a contemporary public. Finally, I will discuss how the new message spills over in the domain of popular culture for commercial consumption.

An Analysis of Tulsī's Phulvārī Episode

Tulsīdās's influential reworking of the Rāma story, the *Rāmcaritmānas,* dates from the last quarter of the sixteenth century and was created in Eastern U.P., in the cities of Benares and Ayodhyā. Its language is old Hindī (Avadhī), which was not only the vernacular of the region Tulsī was working in, but also a well-developed literary idiom by the time he composed *Rāmcaritmānas.* Moreover, as the vernacular of the area where Rāma is supposed to have lived, it, anachronistically, has come to be seen as 'Rāma's mother tongue'.

Tulsī's work has become a widely popular text, sometimes called 'the Bible of north India' and quoted and recited ever more eagerly even today (see esp. Lutgendorf 1991b). The text of this work seems to be fairly stable, with minor manuscript variants, so I chose the most popular 'Vulgate' text as edited by the Gītā Press from Gorakhpur for my basic textual source in this paper.[1] The Flower Garden passage in which Rāma and Sītā fall in love is found in the part on Rāma's youth (Bāla Kāṇḍa 1: 227-36).

The Flower Garden scene is exactly one of the major 'discrepancies' *vis-à-vis* the 'Sanskrit *Rāmāyaṇa*' that Tulsī introduces in his work. It does not seem to occur in any other pre-Tulsī *Rāmāyaṇa,* though the twelfth-century Tamil *Rāmāyaṇa* by Kampan has a pre-marital exchange of glances during Rāma's entrance into Mithilā (see, e.g., Shulman 1994: 98-99). However, the Flower Garden scene had precedents in the *kāvya* tradition. Apparently, Rāma and Sītā falling in love was a well-established topic of dramatic representations of the *Rāmāyaṇa* story. It occurs most notably in Bhavabhūti's eighth-century *Mahāvīracarita,* and Jayadeva II's thirteenth-century

1. It made most sense for the purpose of this paper to stick with the most popular edition, rather than to look at the 'critical' one from Ramcandra Shukla's *Tulsī Granthāvali,* which is at least partly based on manuscript material and notes variants at the end. My references throughout the paper will be to the sequence in the Gītā Press edition (which is occasionally slightly different from Shukla's), counting each 16+16 *mātrā* line as a *caupāī,* rather than, as usual, the double verse.

Prasannarāghava (Vaudeville 1955: 104). Of course, the theme of falling in love (*pūrvarāga*) in itself is a favourite of Sanskrit *belles lettres*, the *kāvya* tradition, in general. In addition, Tulsī may have drawn inspiration also from vernacular models on the theme of first love, such as the tradition of Sūfī romances in Avadhī, which was well-established since at least the fourteenth century. In these texts, the theme of love at first sight is loaded with theological meaning. Tulsī must also have been familiar with the Braj Bhāṣā poetry on the theme of the romances of another mythological hero, namely Kṛṣṇa, which had been coming up in popularity since the end of the fifteenth century. One of the major themes in the new 'hot' Braj literature was the ever-new love of Kṛṣṇa and his favourite Rādhā in a bucolic setting. In order to understand Tulsī's agenda, it pays off to work out in detail how his version of the scene differs from such potential models that he might have been influenced by.

Potential Kāvya Models

In Bhavabhūti's *Mahāvīracarita* (act 1), Rāma and Sītā meet under the auspices of Viśvāmitra at the latter's hermitage. They are in the company of chaperones: Rāma and Lakṣmaṇa are in the retinue of the saint Viśvāmitra, and Sītā and Urmilā have arrived accompanied by their uncle (father's youngest brother) Kuśadhvaja. The meeting is an arranged one: Viśvāmitra has set it up for the sake of arranging the match between the brothers and sisters. There is indication of blossoming romance, though the scene has its share of *vīrya rasa* and solemnity given the meeting between hermit and king. The sisters are immediately interested in the boys and get to express their admiration 'They are handsome to behold!' (*sommadaṁsanā kkhu ede, MC,* 1:19); Sītā confides when hearing about the story of Ahalyā: 'his power is equal to his body's beauty' (*sarīraṇimmāṇasariso se aubhāvo, MC,* 1: 27), and Rāma declares to Lakṣmaṇa that he is enchanted (*utpattir devayajanād brahmavādī nṛpa pitā, suprasannojjvalā mūrtir asyām snehaṁ karoti me, MC,* 1:21).

There is even time for a moment of whispered confidences of brothers: 'What makes this girl cure my eye like a nectar' (*tat kim iyam amṛtavartir iva me cakṣur āpyāyati*), and sisters: 'Why does my gaze attach in this happiness for the eyes' (*kiṁ tti sajjai imassiṁ loaṇāṇande me diṭhṭhī, MC,* 1:29).

However, the *pūrvaranga* theme is relatively undeveloped and the stress is more on *vīrya rasa:* the princes get ample occasion to impress the girls by showing off their strength, as the slaying of Tāṭaka occurs (off the scene) and they receive divine weapons in remuneration. Most importantly, whatever awakening of first love there is, is immediately linked with matrimonial purposes. The act includes (off the scene) the breaking of the bow by Rāma, and ends with the official arrangement of the marriage by the elders.

In the second act of Jayadeva (II)'s *Prasannarāghava,* on the other hand, we find an exclusively romantic treatment. It features the first meeting of both lovers, this time unchapperoned by their elders, though clearly engaged in legitimate activities: Rāma and his brother are in the garden to pick flowers for Viśvāmitra, and Sītā is on her way to worship in the temple. The location here is a blossoming spring garden in Mithilā, with a pond near a goddess temple (Caṇḍikāyatana, *PR,* 2, Shastri and Tripathi 1977: 110). All these elements are the same as in Tulsī's *RCM.*

The second act of this play has been surmised to have been a direct source of inspiration for Tulsī (Vaudeville 1955: 104). Establishing such direct relations between sources remains always hypothetical, and of course we have no evidence that

Tulsī would have had access to the play, let alone to the text of the play as we have it now. That being said, there are tempting similarities, at the level of language as well as plot between Tulsī's and *PR*'s *puṣpavāṭikā* scenes.

One element they have in common comes right at the beginning of the scenes: both authors explicitly stress the setting as romantic. The first words of Jayadeva's Rāma to Lakṣmaṇa upon appearance on the scene are, 'Look, look, what a delightful garden' (*paśya paśyārāmaramaṇīyakam, PR,* 2, Shastri and Tripathi 1977: 106), with a pun that draws attention that the essence of 'pleasure garden' (*ārāma*) is related to 'pleasure', via its underlying verbal root *ram.* Lakṣmaṇa confirms this in his answer:

> *nisargaramaṇīyo 'yam ārāmaḥ* ।
> Naturally beautiful is this garden.

The very same wordplay is echoed in the opening description of the garden in *RCM,* in particular in an important tone-setting *dohā:*

> *bāgu taḍāgu biloki prabhu haraṣe bandhu sameta* ।
> *parama ramya ārāmu yahu jo rāmahi sukhạ deta* ॥
>
> Having seen the tank in the garden, the Lord, rejoiced with his brother. The highest enjoyable garden/ comfort comfort is that, which gives pleasure to Rāma.
>
> — *RCM* 1:227 *doḥā*

Tulsī's *dohā* is richer: in addition to the *ārāma/ram* wordplay, he also plays on the name of Rāma, which is related to the same verbal root. Interestingly, this comes up also in the play *PR,* but a bit later in the act, where Sītā, wandering through the garden, has discovered and is beholding Rāma. At this point, Sītā's girlfriend chides her for being absent-minded and teasingly asks, 'Where then have you turned your mind?' (*kva tarhi dattacittāsi?*, *PR*, 2, Shastri and Tripathi 1977: 132), upon which Sītā cleverly answers with a near-truth: *ārāmammi*, 'to the garden'. The girlfriend, however, quickly picks up on the 'Rāma' hidden in this statement and congratulates Sītā for her quick recovery with another pun: 'Well, well, what cleverness of yours! That you have called in an *ā* to hide your expression (betraying your feelings) of 'Ah!' (*aho te cāturyam yat ākāraprakaṭanenaivākāraguptiṁ kṛtavatsyasi*, *PR*, 2, Shastri and Tripathi 1977: 132).

The commentator explains: 'The meaning is: Where you should have said 'Rāma', you said *ārāma* in an attempt to hide your intention', *rāme iti vaktavye ārāme ityuktvā 'bhiprāya-gopanaceṣṭāṁ kṛtavatyasi iti bhāvā* (Shastri and Tripathi 1977: 133). In the end, Jayadeva has the same significant wordplay as Tulsī. However, his wordplay is less theologically loaded, but functions to underscore the bashfulness of the heroine.

Other striking similarities can be found. In both cases, the brothers first hear the women's anklet jingling before they see them. Rāma says:

> *aye ka eṣa madakalakarikanakaśṛṅkhalāmaṇiraṇitānukārī manohārī ko'pi kalakalaḥ samullasati? tad avaśyam iha salīlacalaccaraṇaraṇanmaṇinūpurayā purāṅganayā kayācana caṇḍikāyatanam āgacchantyābhavitavyam*

> Hey, what beautiful sound resounds, which imitates the rattling of the jewel in the golden chain of an intoxicated elephant? Surely it must be (a sound produced) by a beautiful city-woman going to the Caṇḍikā temple, her jewelled anklets rejoicing at her fluently moving feet.
>
> — *PR*, 2, Shastri and Tripathi 1977: 111

Tulsī's parallel line has a different metaphor but is equally onomatopoeic and erotic:

> *kaṁkana kiṁkinī nūpura dhuni suni, kahata lakhana sana rāmu hṛdayaṁ guni* ।
> *mānahuṁ madana duṁdubhī dīnhī,*
> *manasā bisva bijaya kahaṁ kīnhī* ॥

> Hearing the sound of bracelet, belt, and anklet-bells,
> Rāma said to his brother, pondering over it in his heart:
> 'It is as if the god of love is beating his victory drums
> to announce his intention to conquer the world.'
>
> — *RCM*, 1:230.1-2

It is mainly in their reaction to the women that Jayadeva's and Tulsī's Rāma are similar. When he hears the women approach, Jayadeva's Rāma initially shies away from looking upon 'strange women': 'So enough of our spying in that direction. Even the suspicion of (the presence of) another's woman makes Rāghava shy away' (*tad alam asmākam ito 'valokanena parastṛti śaṅkāpi saṅkocāya raghuṇāṁ*, Shastri and Tripathi 1977: 111). He is, however, inclined to stay and look on when he hears from the girls' talk that it is the king's daughter who is arriving.

Tulsī's Rāma, when he catches a glimpse of Sītā, is troubled about his strong feelings in a similar vein:

> *raghubaṁsinha kara sahaja subhāū, manu kupaṁtha pagu dharai na kāū* ।
> *mohi atisaya pratīti mana kerī, jehiṁ sapanehuṁ paranāri na herī* ॥

> The true nature of Rāghavas is that never they put a foot on the wrong path not (even) mentally. (But here) I feel strong love in my heart, which does not look

> upon another's wife, not even in a dream!
>
> — *RCM*, 1:231.5-6

Also elsewhere Jayadeva's and Tulsī's Rāma have a similar duty-minded characteristic in common. For instance, in the play Rāma interrupts his brother's and his own versifying about the beauty of the garden, to turn to the duty of picking flowers for Viśvāmitra (*PR*, 2, Shastri and Tripathi 1977: 109), and at the end of the act, he again interrupts their poetic musings about the beauty of the evening and the rising moon to take the flowers to their guru (*PR*, 2, Shastri and Tripathi 1977: 148). Tulsī's Rāma too interrupts his musings about the moon to go and pay obeisance to the guru (*gura pahiṁ cale nisā baḍi jānī*, *RCM*, 1:238.4b)

Another significant similarity lies in Sītā's prayer. In the play, just a little while after Rāma first has passed by the goddess temple and paid obeisance, Sītā worships in the shrine, with the words:

> *devi sasaharamaulidehāddhadhāriṇī tribhuaṇadharasuhāsiṇi ṇamo ṇamo de*
>
> — *PR* 2, Shastri and Tripathi 1977: 116

> O goddess, who are half of the body of the god with the moon for crest jewel, who dwells in the mansion of the three worlds.

This address clearly stresses the married and householder status of the goddess. No wonder that Sītā's girlfriend remarks teasingly that these words of Sītā are highly appropriate. This subtle hinting at Sītā's desire for a husband is voiced more explicitly in a prayer by the friend on Sītā's behalf immediately afterwards. The dramatic function of these words is that without having to detract from the shyness and bashfulness of the heroine, the hero is informed that she is of marriageable age and that her heart's desire is to be married.

In *RCM*, only Sītā's second prayer, after she has met Rāma, is reported in detail. Here too, the epithets Sītā uses to address the goddess are related to the goddess's role as wife and mother (e.g., *jaya jaya giribararāja kisorī, jaya mahesa mukha caṁda cakorī, RCM,* 1:235.5) 'Glory to the princess of the Mountain king, Glory to the one glued to Maheśa's moonface like a *cakorī* bird' and the *dohā:*

> *patidevatā sutīya mahiṁ, mātu prathama tava rekha* ।
> *mahimā amita na sakahiṁ kahi, sahasa sāradā seṣa* ॥

> Among women loyal to their husband-gods, mother, your place is foremost; your immeasurable greatness cannot be uttered by a thousand of goddesses of speech or (multi-tongued) Śeṣa. — *RCM,* 1:235

In Tulsī's text, the prayer to the goddess Pārvatī is not overheard by Rāma, but it has another extra dimension. It has to be seen against the background of Tulsī's elaborate retelling of the story of Śiva and Pārvatī in the beginning of his Bāla-Kāṇḍa, which is just one of the many instances where Tulsī seems to be engaged in an ecumenical effort, integrating Śaiva elements within his essentially Vaiṣṇava story (Hawley and Juergensmeyer 1988: 153-55).

Though there is no danger of being overheard, like Jayadeva II's, Tulsī's Sītā too is shy in voicing explicitly her desire. Instead, she humbly prays:

> *mora manorathu jānahu nīkeṁ, basahu sadā ura pura sabhī keṁ* ।
>
> *kīnheuṁ pragaṭa na kārana tehīṁ, asa kahi carana gahe baidehīṁ* ॥

> 'You know well my heart's desire, because you eternally dwell in everyone's heart. So, I haven't openly told you the reason (for my prayer)' saying such, the princess of Videha clasped the feet (of the goddess image). — *RCM*, 1:236.3-4

This unassuming humble prayer is immediately received favourably with a little miraculous sign of approval: 'Bhavānī was swayed by this humble love, she slipped down a flower garland and the image smiled' (*vinaya prema basa bhaī bhavānī, khasī māla mūrati musukānī*, *RCM*, 1:236.5). This is significant, as it reveals Tulsī's general *bhakti* agenda with its message that selfless love towards god will be answered in kind.

A final strong similarity comes at the end of the act, where both Tulsī and Jayadeva II have their hero poetically muse about their feelings while the moon rises in the evening sky. In the play, when the girls are gone, Rāma composes a verse, comparing Sītā to the moon, and Lakṣmaṇa announces the arrival of the night and the moon with a double-entendre verse, which can also be understood to refer to Sītā (*PR*, 2:31, Shastri and Tripathi 1977: 142). The brothers poetically continue to describe the sky's beauty: Rāma appropriately points out how the moon makes lovers suffer in separation (*PR* 2:34, Shastri and Tripathi 1977: 145); Lakṣmaṇa ends on a positive note. Some of the mythological imagery in these verses seems echoed (though with different meaning) in Tulsī's *RCM* where Rāma compares Sītā to the moon, yet corrects himself, realising how none of the flaws of the moon are apparent in his blameless beloved (see, e.g., references to the ocean of milk: *dugdhābdhibandhu*, *PR*, 2:35c and *janamu siṁdhu puni baṁdhu viṣu*, *RCM*, 1:27 *dohā*)

While the similarities are striking, we have already noted some ways in which Tulsī's version deviates from

Prasannarāghava in the very passages that seem parallel. Other major general differences are also to be noted. For one, Tulsī's hero is not half as poetic in spouting erotic verse, as is Jayadeva's. Most importantly, Jayadeva's Sītā, though bashful, expresses her feelings in similar erotic verse directed to her girlfriends, e.g., where she catches a first glimpse of Rāma, she calls him 'destroyer of the beauty of Cupid', or *anaṅgarūpakhaṇḍaṇa* (*PR*, 2:21, Shastri and Tripathi 1977: 130). Tulsī's heroine, by contrast, does not seem to speak a single word during the whole scene. The corresponding verse in *RCM* (1:233) is a *nakha-śikha* description of the boys, with similar phrases (*jo biloki bahu kāma lajāhīṁ* 'upon seeing him, many Cupids are ashamed', *RCM*, 1:233.6b).[2] However, this verse is not put in Sītā's mouth, but seems to be the joined comments of the girlfriends (cf. the concluding *dohā:* 'Having seen the jewel of the Sun dynasty, the girlfriends totally forgot themselves' *dekhi bhānukulabhūṣanahi, bisarā sakhinha apān*). Whereas the girlfriend of Jayadeva's Sītā addresses Lakṣmaṇa directly (*PR*, 2, Shastri and Tripathi 1977: 123), Tulsī's girls only speak among themselves, (though at times with the intent to be overheard, to be sure, cf. *RCM*, 1:234.6a *puni āuba ehi beriāṁ kālī* 'We'll come back same time tomorrow'*)*. Finally, Jayadeva's Rāma addresses Sītā directly (*PR*, 2:22, Shastri and Tripathi 1977: 133), asking her to look up at him, in very poetic language. She does not answer him directly, but addresses several poetic erotic verses to her friend, and finally does look up. In Tulsī's text, on the other hand, the hero and heroine do not exchange a single word. One of Sītā's girlfriends encourages her to look into Rāma's eyes:

---

2. Another similarity in these lines is the reference to Rāma sporting a peacock feather in his hair: *śikhaṇḍamaṇḍana, PR,* 2:21d *morapaṅkha sira sohata nīke, RCM,* 1:233.2a.

> *dhari dhīraju eka āli sayānī, sītā sana bolī gahi pānī, bahuri gauri kara dhyāna karehū, bhūpakisora dekhi kina lehū* ।
> *sakuci sīyaṁ taba nayana ughāre, sanamukha dou raghusiṁgha nihāre* ॥
>
> Taking courage, one clever girl-friend, took Sītā by the hand and said: 'You will meditate on Gaurī again (later), why don't you take a look at the princes (now)' hesitatingly Sītā then opened her eyes, and gazed at the two lions of the Raghu family in front of her.
>
> — *RCM* 1:234.1-3

Such differences, where Jayadeva voices and Tulsī describes feelings are to a large part due to the difference in genre. Jayadeva has to make everything explicit for the audience in the words of the characters themselves. However, Tulsī's tendency to de-eroticise the text is also reinforced by the lack of interaction between Sītā and Rāma.

Another difference is that in Jayadeva's play, it is Rāma who is observing the girls hidden in the bushes, until Sītā 'discovers' him. In Tulsī's version, Rāma and Lakṣmaṇa see the women first, but the women are the ones who have set out to spy on the princes. They are led by one 'explorer' girlfriend:

> *eka sakhī siya saṁgu bihāī, gaī rahī dekhana phulavāī* ।
> *tehiṁ dou baṁdhu biloke jāī, prema bibasa sītā pahiṁ āī* ॥
>
> — *RCM*, 1:228.7-8, see also dohā and 229

and hide in the bushes to get a good look at the men:

> *latā oṭa saba sakhinha lakhāe, syāmala gaura kisora suhāe*
>
> All her friends showed her from the cover of the creepers, the beautiful dark and fair prince.
>
> — *RCM*, 1:232.3

In the play, dramatic action has its own exigencies. The audience's expectation is built up in crescendo: Sītā first sees Lakṣmaṇa, and immediately feels motherly towards him, which she explicitly calls *vātsalya bhāva* ['Seeing him, my heart becomes cleansed with motherly love, as if for my own dear (younger relative)' *imaṁ pekkhantīe maha ṇiavacchasmi via vacchattaṇapacchāliaṁ hi aaṁ vaṭṭadi*, *PR*, 2, Shastri and Tripathi 1977: 122.] Lakṣmaṇa has similar feelings towards her, seeing her as a mother. Sītā, futhermore, immediately links him with Urmilā, at which point the girlfriend cleverly surmises that there must be another man around, who could be coupled to Sītā. However, the audience's expectation of an imminent meeting between Rāma and Sītā is postponed by Sītā herself, who decides that it is not good to linger and declares she'll go home. Luckily, she then changes her mind to look at one of her favourite trees, a mango which is embraced by the *Vāsantī* creeper. When the girls reach the spot where Rāma was standing just a minute ago, Sītā 'reads the traces in the tree' and detects the presence of a lover nearby (Shastri and Tripathi 1977: 125). More suggestive botanic imagery is to follow in poetic musings of the girlfriend and Rāma (to himself), before Rāma and Sītā finally behold one another.

Tulsī's text, on the other hand, is totally devoid of such erotic botanic imagery. The plot development is much more straightforward, and there is no question at all of Urmilā, all action is concentrated on the meeting of Rāma and Sītā only.

In Jayadeva's play, an external interruption is necessary as a ploy to end the scene, with the arrival of a servant of Sītā's mother who calls her back to the palace (Shastri and Tripathi 1977: 139). Whereas in Tulsī's text, it is her own girlfriends, who, upon realising how lost she is, remind her of the lateness of the hour (*parabasa sakhinha lakhī jaba sītā, bhayau gaharu saba kahahiṁ sabhītā, RCM,* 1:234.5). The girlfriends here function very much like in the Braj poems on Rādhā and Kṛṣṇa where it is their task to bring the lovers together, but also to ensure they do not get totally absorbed in each other when together.

In general, then, Tulsī's text is more static, the stress is on Rāma and Sītā's mutual beholding rather than how the beholding gets to come about, as in the play. Here we put again our finger on Tulsī's theological agenda. The *phulvārī* scene clearly is set-up such that Sītā becomes a model for the human devotee or *bhakta,* and it stresses an important aspect of human-divine contact: visual experience or *darśana.* The contact between Tulsī's lovers in the passage is purely limited to seeing each other. As we have seen, they do not engage in any verbal interchange, let alone in physical contact (as would be the case in erotic *kāvya* poetry).

Most of the action in Tulsī is limited to, or better, concentrated on Sītā seeing Rāma and Rāma seeing Sītā. A lot of attention is devoted to Sītā's gazing upon the divine beloved:

> *dekhi rūpa locana lalacāne, haraṣe janu nija nidhi pahicāne* ।
> *thake nayana raghupati chabi dekheṁ, palakanhihūṁ pariharīṁ nimeṣeṁ* ॥

> Seeing his beauty, her eyes became eager, they rejoiced as if they had recognised their own (lost) treasure. Her eyes grew tired, gazing at Raghupati's appearance, blinking left her very eyelids.
>
> — *RCM,* 1:232.4-5

Tulsī describes the psychological effect in detail, by means of directly 'reading her mind':

adhika sanehaṁ deha bhai bhorī, sarada sasihi janu citava cakorī ।
locana maga rāmahi ura ānī, dīnhe palaka kapāṭa sayānī ॥
— *RCM*, 1:232.6-7

Her body became unaware in the overdose of love, like a partridge gazing at the autumn moon. By the pathway of her eyes, she led Rāma in her heart, then closed the door of her eyelids, the clever girl.

However, Tulsī's 'camera' does not remain stuck on the devotee: it shifts back and forth from Sītā to Rāma.

asa kahi phiri citae tehi orā, siya mukha sasi bhae nayana cakorā ।
— *RCM*, 1:230.3

Saying such, he then glanced in that direction, Sītā's face became the moon, his eyes partidges.

karata batakahī anuja sana, mana siya rūpa lobhāna ।
mukha saroja makaraṁda chabi, karai madhupa iva pāna ॥
— *RCM*, 1:231 *dohā*

While he was discoursing with his younger brother, his mind was eager for Sītā's beauty. He drunk the beauty of her face like a bee the pollen of a lotus.

And Rāma's psychological response is reported, either in description:

bhae bilocana cāru acaṁcala, manahuṁ sakuci nimi taje digaṁcala ।
dekhi sīya sobhā sukhu pāvā, hṛdayaṁ sarāhata bacanu na āvā ॥
— *RCM*, 1:230.4-5

His beautiful eyes remained unblinking, as if Nimi (the forefather of Janaka) had shyly left his eyelids, seeing

> Sītā's beauty he attained bliss. He found no words to praise her in his heart.

Or via the stratagem of his reporting to his brother-confidant, Lakṣmaṇa (*RCM*, 1:231, where he confesses he is attracted, and points out that attraction to a 'strange woman' is impossible for a Rāghava, as quoted already above).

To some extent the stress on the looking in each other's eyes is also there in *Prasannarāghava* (2:22, 25-8, Shastri and Tripathi 1977: 133-38) where a series of verses on the theme of looking are pronounced by Rāma, the girlfriend, and Sītā herself, with the aim of freezing the moment in time. As Rāma himself puts it in the last verse: *api bhavatu sadā 'yaṁ sanmuhūrttaḥ* (*PR*, 2:28c). However, contrary to what is the case in the play, and would be the case in other *kāvya* models, Tulsī describes mainly the beauty of his hero, Rāma, with a full *nakha-śikha* description (*RCM*, 1: 233), not that of the heroine Sītā, who is only eulogised with some general comparisons and the formulaic inability to express her beauty in words (*RCM*, 1: 230.6-8). In the play on the other hand, Rāma gets significantly more airing time on feminine beauty (*PR*, 2: 7-9, Shastri and Tripathi 1977: 112 and 114-15; *PR*2: 11-12, Shastri and Tripathi 1977: 117 and 119; *PR*, 2: 16-17, Shastri and Tripathi 1977: 124 and 126; *PR*, 2: 19-20, Shastri and Tripathi 1977: 128-29) than Sītā does (*PR*, 2: 21, Shastri and Tripathi 1977: 130).

Tulsī clearly has designed his scene according to his *bhakti* agenda, with a strong focus on beholding the divine. Nevertheless, this agenda also involves reciprocity and the certainty of god's response to the devotee's sincere love, as has been noticed by the commentators (Śaran 1925: 350-51), Tulsī makes it a point to stress the complete reciprocity between lover and beloved. Significantly, immediately after the meeting scene, both are portrayed as reflecting upon their love for each other. Sītā has a hard time leaving (she turns her head back to behold Rāma on the slightest pretext, *RCM*, 1:234 *dohā*) and is portrayed as worrying about Rāma's capacity to pass the test of the bow, the condition for her marriage.

> *jāni kaṭhina sivacāpa bisūrati, calī rākhi ura syāmala mūratī* ।
>
> Knowing how tough Śiva's bow was, she became distressed, she left with his dark image in her heart.

The next scene has her ardently pray in the Girijā temple 'that her wish may come true' (*RCM*, 1:235.1). Rāma hates to see her leave too (*RCM*, 1:235.2-3) and he is portrayed as romantically musing upon his beloved's beauties at night, taking the pretext of reflecting on a poetic comparison with the moon (*RCM*, 1:237-8.1-4). In the latter scene, the influence of the Sanskritic *kāvya* poetic tradition is obvious. When Rāma reproaches himself for even daring to compare Sītā's beauty with that of the moon, he uses the figure of speech of *vyatireka,* where the traditional object of comparison is one-upped by its subject. More in particular, the scene is reminiscent of the final dialogue of Rāma and Lakṣmaṇa in the second act of *PR,* where they poetically describe the beauty of the evening and the moon in romantic terms (see above).

There are, in short, many elements in common between *RCM* and *PR* that are instructive for a comparison. However, regardless of whether this exact play was the source or not, it is clear that Tulsī draws upon the Sanskrit *kāvya* tradition (as already noted by Vaudeville 1955: 105). What is interesting to us is that, in applying the esthetic theme of *pūrvarāga,* 'first love', to Rāma and Sītā, he is also pushing a particular *bhakti* agenda. Apart from the difference of medium — dramatic action versus poetic description — several transformations can be understood in the light of Tulsī's agenda. Tulsī's main concern is to set-up an example of an ideal relation between devotee and god, and to stress the importance of 'beholding', or *darśana* in that relationship. This involves mainly pondering on god's beauty, but also an element of reciprocity, since god answers the sincere devotee's love. The latter is illustrated both in Pārvatī's answer to Sītā's prayer and in Rāma's returning her feelings. Appropriately for this *bhakti* agenda, the tone is less erotic and playful, but more serene and serious compared to that in *kāvya*.

Vernacular Models

Tulsī is, however, not solely drawing upon Sanskrit sources. One of the major accomplishments of his retelling is, after all, that it is in the vernacular, in Avadhī. By the time Tulsī composed his work, there were already several Avadhī 'romances' available, most of them Sūfī in inspiration. In several of them the theme of 'first love' is described, featuring a meeting between the lovers, chaperoned not by elders, only by their retinue. Often the meeting takes place near a temple, usually during a publicly celebrated festival. However, in the Sūfī romances the heroes regularly faint at such encounters before even the lovers' glances meet. The heroines, on the other hand, tend to be quite bold in the expression of their feelings. Interestingly too, such meetings are portrayed as pre-arranged furtively by well-wishers of the hero and heroine. The hero is frequently disguised as a holy man and has had to practice patience for a long time before the meeting takes place.

It is again not possible to establish whether Tulsī actually had access to the Sūfī romances, and if so, in which form. However, to flesh the aforementioned points out, let us look at some concrete examples of Sūfī *premākhyāna*, or romance, as we know them now.

One of the earliest preserved *premākhyāna*s is Maulānā Dāūd's *Cāndāyana* (dated 1379). Here, the hero Lorik, dressed as Gorakh-panthī has been waiting for a year at a local temple and then faints upon seeing his beloved Cāndā at the temple during Divālī, as arranged by her maid Bṛhaspati. Cāndā tries to revive him, but to no avail (*kaḍavak* 165-69, Gupta 1967: 161-65).[3] When Lorik wakes up, immediately following the incident, he finds himself utterly alone and talks to the deity (unspecified *deva*), who explains what happened (*kaḍavak* 170-71, Gupta 1967: 165-67). Meanwhile Cāndā is confiding her feeling to her maid, with some similarities to the description of Sītā's feelings in *RCM:*

> *naina paisi cita kītesi ṭhāūṁ, bāju kīnha hauṁ anata na jāūṁ* ।
>
> Having entered through my eyes, he found a place in my heart. He took my arm, I won't go elsewhere.[4]
>
> — C, 174 *caupāī*, Gupta 1967: 179

Compare with:

> *locana maga rāmahi ura ānī, dīnhe palaka kapāṭa sayānī* ।
>
> She led Rāma into her heart by way of her eyes, and cleverly closed the door of her eyelids.
>
> — *RCM*, 1:232.7

3. Strictly speaking, this is not their first meeting. Cāndā's maid, Bṛhaspati, had pointed out to Cāndā the handsome young man during his triumphant parade through Govar, whereupon Cāndā had fallen hopelessly in love (*kaḍavak* 135-40, Gupta 1967: 132-37). Upon her maid's advice, Cāndā then had Lorik invited to her father's house for a banquet, at which he sees her for the first time and faints (*kaḍavak* 153, Gupta 1967: 149). I am grateful to Dr. Naseem Hines of University of Washington for directing me to this scene of *Cāndāyana*.
4. I am grateful to Dr. Naseem Hines for helping me with the translation of this line.

An important difference though is that in *RCM* these feelings are not explicitly voiced by Sītā, it is merely the description of what she feels. Tulsī's Sītā is, in other words, much more bashful than the Sūfī romance heroine.

Another even closer parallel occurs in Jāyasī's *Padmāvat* (1540-41). Here, the spring festival is the occasion for Padmāvatī, the princess of Siṅghala, to go to the local Viśvanātha temple with her married girlfriends. There is revelry in a flower garden (*phulvārī, P,* 20:2 *dohā*), and a temple scene where the heroine prays to the image, voicing her desire for a suitable husband. This scene is very similar to the one in *RCM,* quoted above.

> *lei seṁdura āge bhaiṁ kharī, parasi deva puni pāyanha parī* ।
> *aura sahelī sabai biyāhīṁ, mo kahaṁ deva katahuṁ bara nāhīṁ* ॥
> *hauṁ niraguna jei kīnha na sevā, guni niraguni dātā tuma devā* । — *P,* 20:9.5-7

She came forth with vermillion, touched the image and fell at its feet. 'All other girlfriends have married, but, god, for me there's no groom anywhere? I am without virtue, not having performed your service, but you grant virtue to the virtueless, god.'

> *bara sauṁ joga mohiṁ meravahu, kalasa jāti hauṁ māni* ।
> *jehi dina hīchā pūjai, begi caṛhāvahuṁ āni* ॥
> — *P,* 20:9 *dohā*

> *hīṁchi hīṁchi binavā jasa bānī, puni kara jori ṭhāṛhi bhai rānī* । — *P,* 20:10.1

'Arrange for a union of me with a groom, I vow a pitcher (*kalaśa*) (before) I leave. The day my wish comes

> true, I will immediately come and offer it.' Expressing her wish again and again, in words like a prayer, joining her hands, the queen stood up.[5]
>
> — *P*, 10:10.1

However, in this case, the god does not give any reassuring signs. Rather, Padmāvatī suspects 'the god is dead' (*deva mari gaeu*, *P*, 10:10.2) and a thundering voice confirms her thinking. The arrival of Padmāvatī and her beautiful maidens had created such havoc that all the temple servants and indeed the gods themselves had totally lost it.

The Sūfī romance diverges even more from *RCM* from this point onwards. One of Padmāvatī's girlfriends then notifies the heroine of the fact that the leader of a group of *yogī*s in the eastern portico has also fainted, and she suggests that he is not a *bonafide yogī* but a prince who might have come in pursuit of Padmāvatī herself. Padmāvatī, like Cāndā, is unsuccesful in her efforts to revive the hero-holy man, but she leaves a bold message written on his chest.

> *taba caṁdana ākhara hiya likhe, bhīkha lei tui joga na sikhe* ।
> *gharī āi tava gā tū soī, kaiṁse bhuguti parāpati hoī* ।
> *aba jauṁ sūra ahau sasi rātā, āeu caṛhi mo gagana puni sātā* ।
>
> — *P*, 10:13.3-5

> Then she wrote in letters of sandal on his chest: 'You have not learned the *yoga* of taking alms! The hour has come, then you fell asleep, how can you obtain enjoyment. Now, if the sun is attracted to this moon, come to me, climbing the seven heavens.'

Needless to say that such boldness would be quite out of

5. A translation of the work can also be found in Shirreff 1944.

character with shy Sītā in Tulsī's Flower Garden scene. And of course, Rāma does not faint at all. The fainted Sūfī heroes (both Lorik and Ratansen) are described as utterly alone, having no one to come to their rescue. The heroines, by contrast (both Padmāvatī and Cāndā), can speak freely with their confidantes and are comforted by the assurance that union with the beloved is now not far off.

Clearly there was no dearth of precedents for writing on the theme in Avadhī, and the similarities are striking. The setting of a flower garden in spring is very similar to that in Jāyasī. The temple scene where Sītā prays for a suitable husband (*nija anurūpa subhaga baru māgā, RCM,* 1:228.6b) is highly reminiscent of Padmāvatī's prayer. However, whereas Padmāvatī laughs when she hears the gods are not available to help her, Sītā is most serious and shown as very devout (*pūjā kīnha adhika anurāgā, RCM,* 1:228.6a).

Another interesting point may be noted here. The imagery of the union of sun and moon, so prominent in the Sūfī romances, has a vague echo at the end of Rāma's monologue comparison of Sītā with the moon, where his brother compares him with the sun. Significantly though, they are both cases of *vyatireka*. Sītā and Rāma surpass moon and sun in all ways.

More instructive, indeed, than the similarities are the differences. Tulsī's lovers meet without pre-arranged intent, unexpectedly, by sheer coincidence. Though the season of spring heightens the erotic mood, each of the heroes is on a mission of duty, rather than sheer revelry, Sītā acts shy and abashed, in contrast to the heroines of the Sūfī romances.

Whereas Padmāvatī and Cāndā engage with their retinue in merry-making in abandon (*Holī* in the case of Padmāvatī), Sītā and her friends merely sing songs (*gāvahiṁ gīta manohara bānīṁ, RCM,* 1:228.3) and take a bath in the pond (*majjanu kari sara sakhinha sametā, RCM,* 1:228.5), all more serene religious activities.

In general, it seems that Sūfī heroines are less bashful and shy, and their suitors more prone to fainting, at least upon first meeting. The heroes also have to endure more. They suffer through long, intense periods of ordeal, waiting for the desired meeting. Obviously this is connected to the fact that the allegorical value of the Sūfī romance is the opposite of that of Rāma and Sītā: the Sūfī hero stands for the spiritual seeker, who has to go through different stages before he reaches his goal. In the *bhakti* tradition, the heroine is the model for the human devotee, or *bhakta,* and beholding the divine plays a major role in the worship.

If the Avadhī romances were a source of inspiration for Tulsī, it seems, they mainly were so in terms of form. Obviously, Tulsī's work has the same basic metrical structure as the romances, namely, the *kaḍavak* with its alternations between several *caupāī* lines of 16+16 morae or *mātrās* and a final *dohā* of 13+11 *mātrās*. The *dohā* usually sums up the action or mood described in the previous *caupāī*'s and functions as a moment of 'crystallisation' of the emotion. Still, it is instructive to study how potential parallel scenes, set pieces, one could say, differ. The main reason seems to be Tulsī's particular *bhakti* agenda.

This brings us to a second set of vernacular potential models for Tulsī's scene, inspired by a similar *bhakti* agenda. Tulsī could not have failed to be influenced by the literary developments in a closely related vernacular, Braj Bhāṣā. From the late fifteenth century onwards an abundance of devotional literature was being created in this idiom on the theme of the romances of another mythological hero, namely Kṛṣṇa. One of the major themes in the new Braj literature was indeed, just like Tulsī's own, *bhakti*. However, the Braj poetry celebrated the love of Kṛṣṇa and his favourite Rādhā in a bucolic setting. Poets created countless songs on the theme, guided by esthetic categories, such as *pūrvarāga*. By the end of the sixteenth century, when Tulsī was composing his *Rāmcaritmānas*, such Braj devotional songs had become widely popular. Tulsī's decision to add the *phulvārī* scene on the first love of Rāma and Sītā may well have been inspired by the countless, very popular examples of Braj Bhāṣā Rādhā and Kṛṣṇa songs.

Given the wide diversity of songs on this theme, it is a huge task to try and sort out which particular ones might have been direct sources of inspiration for Tulsī. And again, the exercise may be fruitless, in that it remains impossible to establish such lines of influence with any certainty. As is the case with Avadhī, the very use of the same or a similar idiom ensures that the poetry will have certain oral formulaic expressions in common.

Given the fact that both Tulsī and the Braj poets are working within the *bhakti* tradition, they will unavoidably share certain typical *bhakti* thematic elements. One could be the *maṇḍala*-style setting of the romance. Tulsī's flower garden is not merely a device for creating a romantic mood, as it was for Jayadeva in his play. Like the bucolic scenes of Rādhā and Kṛṣṇa poetry, it is a setting of theological significance. The garden is a highly structured landscape which functions as a diagram for meditation. It is, so to speak, a temple in the centre of which the beholding of divinity can take place. This is made clear at the very beginning of the scene, where the flower garden is described as having a pond in its centre.

> *madhya bāga saru soha suhāvā, mani sopāna bicitra banāvā* ।

bimala salilu sarsija bahuraṁgā, jalakhaga kūjata guṁjata bhṛṁgā ॥

In the middle of the garden, shone a beautiful lake, constructed with jewelled steps. There was pure water, colourful lotuses, warbling waterbirds and buzzing bees. — *RCM*, 1:227.4

This description is reminiscent of settings for Rādhā and Kṛṣṇa poetry, in the imaginary Braj-scape. In particular, one is reminded of the poetry set near so-called Mānasarovar, a magic pond in the Braj world. Of course, in Tulsī's work there is an extra dimension. After all, the title of Tulsī's work means, 'the holy lake of the acts of Rāma'. In this context the pond with its steps has a very specific deep theological meaning (see Lutgendorf 1991a: 18-29). Its occurrence, then, at this important moment in the story is doubly significant.

Whether there was indeed direct influence of specific models in Braj for Tulsī's work, is less important a question. The main similarity is clear: Tulsī, like the Braj poets, is concerned with casting Sanskritic esthetics into a vernacular devotional mould. Love between woman and man becomes the metaphor for love between human and divine. Tulsī's main agenda is clearly one of *bhakti:* stressing the complete reciprocity of human and divine in love, with mutual *darśana* as the cornerstone, and in that respect, he is on the same wavelength as Kṛṣṇa *bhakti.*

However, it is also obvious that Tulsī chooses very explicitly to distance himself from the more overtly erotic Kṛṣṇa *bhakti* scenes. We have already noted that Tulsī studiously avoids physical contact between the lovers, which contrasts, not only with the Sūfī and *kāvya* poems, but also with the bulk of the Rādhā-Kṛṣṇa material. Connected with this is the different framing of the whole scene. Much of the Braj materials derive part of their charm from titillation of the more or less explicit secrecy of the tryst and its exciting, if not downright adulterous, at least illegitimate nature. Tulsī on the other hand seems nearly obsessively concerned with assuring his public of the legitimacy of the meeting. Whereas the Kṛṣṇa *bhakti* stresses the aspect of eroticism, *śṛṅgāra,* Tulsī makes sure to drench the whole episode in a tone of *maryādā,* or conventional morality.

Tulsī accomplishes his goal by repeated steps in the direction of legitimising the pre-marital love of Rāma and Sītā. All possible titillation that might be associated with a scene featuring voyeurism, or at least girls looking at boys and vice versa is carefully eradicated. Tulsī succeeds in his purpose of keeping sweet first love within the limits of *maryādā* in several ways.

First of all he makes sure the public is abundantly aware that the protagonists' presence at the scene is totally legitimate, in fact even ordered by their elders. Rāma and Lakṣmaṇa are in the garden to pick flowers for worshipping their *guru*. They had obtained the *guru*'s explicit blessing to do so:

> *samaya jāi gura āyasu pāī, lena prasūna cale dou bhāī* ||
>
> With an eye to the auspicious event (of *guru-pūjā*), both brothers obtained their *guru*'s permission to go and pick flowers. — *RCM*, 1:227.1b

Tulsī even makes it clear they also got permission to pick flowers from the garderners themselves:

> *cahuṁ disi citai pūṁchi mālīgana, lage lena dala phūla mudita mana* |
>
> They searched in all directions, asked the gardeners,

> and started to collect flowers and petals with reassured hearts. — *RCM*, 1:228.1

In other words, Tulsī is concerned in portraying the brothers as not just 'hanging out' in the place. He does the same for Sītā and her girlfriends. They got explicit orders from Sītā's mother to go and worship the goddess whose temple is in the garden:

> *tehi avasara sītā tahaṁ āī, girijā pūjana janani paṭhāī* ।

> At that moment Sītā arrived there, sent by her mother to worship Pārvatī. — *RCM*, 1: 228.2

Further, neither Rāma nor Sītā are active agents in bringing the meeting about. They are portrayed as totally innocent, the meeting is absolutely by chance and in no way do they steer towards it. It is one of the more adventurous girlfriends of Sītā who takes the initiative to go and look at the boys and drag the other girls along (*RCM*, 1:228.7-8 and *dohā*, 229). Sītā timidly joins her friends but only because she knows this is her 'old love'. She is reminded of Nārada's prediction to the effect that she will marry Rāma, since they are incarnations of Lakṣmī and Viṣṇu (the prediction itself is not related in *RCM*, as discussed by Vaudeville 1955: 105-6). Consequently, Tulsī hastens to add, it is pure love (*prīti punīta*).

> *calī agra kari priya sakhi soī, prīti purātana lakhai na koī* ।
> *sumiri sīya nārada vacana upajī prīti punīta, cakita bilokati sakala disi janu sisu mr̥gī sabhīta* ॥

> That same dear girlfriend was made to lead, and they left. No one can know old love. Sītā remembered Nārada's prediction, which inspired a pure love. Agitated she looked in all directions, like a frightened little fawn. — *RCM*, 1:229.8 and *dohā*

As we have pointed out above, Rāma is similarly confused about the strength of his feelings when he sees the girls. Not only does Tulsī's Rāma feel compelled to reflect on his 'sinful' feelings, but he confesses them to his brother:

> *siya sobhā hiyaṁ barani prabhu, āpani dasā bicāri* ।
> *bole suci mana anuja sana, bacana samaya anuhāri* ॥

> Praising Sītā's beauty in his heart, the Lord pondered over his own mental state. With pure mind, he spoke to his younger brother words that befit the occasion.
>
> — *RCM*, 1:230 *dohā*

Tulsī clearly is eager to stress Rāma's purity of mind (*suci mana*). Rāma then goes on to communicate to his brother how his usually unperturbed mind is now in commotion (*sahaja punīta mora manu chobhā*, *RCM*, 1:231.3b). It is not proper for a Rāghava to be so perturbed at the sight of 'strange' women (*RCM*, 1:231). Rāma here implicitly justifies his love by reasoning that he, unblemishable as he is, cannot possibly be feeling what he does for a woman who is not his own, so this must be the wife predestined for him.

Clearly, Tulsī feels compelled to justify even the 'passively going along' aspect of the chance meeting of his protagonists. They both have an inkling that this person is no 'stranger' but rather the bride/groom to be, and even the intimately close marital partner from previous births, or rather, from their true divine identities as Lakṣmī and Viṣṇu.

Such concerns of Tulsī are not random and stand in strong contrast to the Rādhā-Kr̥ṣṇa mythology, where there has been a strong hint of the adulterous. Rādhā is often understood as married to another (*parakīyā*), though this is in fact a hotly debated issue (De 1961: 348-51). However, in Tulsī's Sītā's case, there is no ambiguity possible. Sītā is safely and soundly Rāma's own (*svakīyā*).

Next, Tulsī ensures legitimacy by avoiding any hint of licentiousness in the meeting itself. Rather, even the visual contact is squarely within the bounds of propriety. There is no question of the flirting, fleeting sidelong glances (*kaṭākṣa*), so celebrated in Sanskrit *kāvya* on the topic. Instead, we could speak of a stability of the gaze, clearly pointing to the theological concept of a steady *darśana*. Rāma's gaze is *acañcala* (*RCM*, 1:222.4), Sītā's eyes stop blinking (*palakanhihuṁ pariharīṁ nimeṣeṁ*, *RCM*, 1:232.5c). In fact, Sītā is so overcome that she even closes her eyes (*RCM*, 1:232.7).

Again this has theological significance: Tulsī has married the typical *bhakti* theology of *darśana* with an older more *yoga* oriented idea of meditation or *dhyāna*. Significantly, Sītā has her eyes closed through the whole *nakha-śikha* description of the princes to follow (*RCM*, 1:233). She does not open her eyes until her friends lure her out of this state of meditation by encouraging her to meditate on the man before her eyes 'instead of meditating on the goddess' (*RCM*, 1:234.2 already quoted above).

In putting it this way, the girls interpret Sītā's closure of the eyes as a devotional act, which again heightens the atmosphere of *maryādā* instead of *śṛṅgāra*. Again, when Sītā finally allows herself a good look at Rāma's beauty from head to toe (*nakha-śikha*), she immediately interrupts her thoughts by 'remembering' her father's oath, namely that she will marry only the one who can break the bow (*nakha sikha dekhi rāma kai sobhā, sumiri pitā panu manu ati chobhā*, *RCM*, 234.4).

Significantly too, neither of the protagonists tries actively to prolong the meeting. Again, passivity prevails. Both parties are so overcome by feeling that they become 'stunned' and 'immobile'. The girlfriends once again take the initiative and drag Sītā away, dropping a clever hint suggesting a possible future rendezvous (*RCM*, 1:234.5-6), and Sītā immediately thinks of her mother's worry if she'd be late (*bhayau bilaṁbu mātu bhaya mānī*, *RCM*, 1:234.7) and is well aware she's in her father's care (*phirī apanapau pitubasa jāne*, *RCM*, 1:234.8). However, Sītā, touchingly, shows some regret, when she follows the Sanskrit *kāvya* tradition in looking back at Rāma on some pretext or other:

> *dekhata misa mr̥ga bihaga taru, phiraī bahori bahori* ।
> *nirakhi nirakhi raghubīra chabi, bāḍhai prīti na thori* ॥

> With the excuse of looking at a deer, a bird, a tree, she turned back again and again. Gazing at the Raghu hero's beauty, her love grew in no small measure.
>
> — *RCM*, 1:234 *dohā*

Finally, after the meeting, the two lovers do not let go of their composure, not even in the privacy of their thoughts. Sītā goes to the temple to pray for a husband, but, as mentioned before, she does not even express her wish that this might be Rāma explicitly in her thoughts, stressing the goddess knows her heart anyway (*RCM*, 1:236.4, already quoted).

To further ensure the propriety of Sītā's feelings for her totally 'suitable' boy, Tulsī arranges for nothing less than a miraculous divine sanction. We have already seen how the image smiled and shed a flower garland as a sign (*RCM*, 1:236.5) Tulsī also has the goddess speak her approval very explicitly:

> *sādara siyaṁ prasādu sira dhareū, bolī gauri harașu hiyaṁ bhareū* ।
> *sunu siya satya asīsa hamārī, pūjihi mana kāmanā tumhārī* ॥

> Sītā reverently touched the garland of grace (*prasāda*) against her head. Joy filled her heart, as the goddess spoke: 'Listen Sītā, my blessing is true, your heart's desire will be fulfilled.' — *RCM*, 1:236.6-7

And to ensure total propriety, the goddess too refers to Nārada's prediction as a sanctifier of this love:

> *nārada bacana sadā suci sācā, so baru milihi jāhiṁ manu rācā* ।
>
> Nārada's words are always pure truth. You will obtain the bridegroom to whom your heart is attached.
> — *RCM* 1:236.8

Tulsī does not leave it at that and elaborates on the business of divine sanction even further in a following *chanda* and *dohā*.

Rāma is equally dutiful and does not let his newly awakened love get in the way of his duties in serving his *guru*. Indeed, Rāma has duly reported the incident to his elder, as Tulsī puts it: so pure is his character that deceit cannot touch it:

> *rāma kahā sabu kausika pāhīṁ, sarala subhāu chuata chala nāhīṁ* । — *RCM*, 1:237.2
>
> Just as Sītā got divine sanction from the goddess, Rāma receives the blessing of his *guru*.

> *sumana pāi muni pūjā kīnhī, puni asīsa duhu bhāinha dīnhī* ।
> *suphala manorath hohuṁ tumhāre, rāmu lakhanu suni bhae sukhāre* ॥ — *RCM*, 1:237.3-4

Rāma dutifully discharges all his tasks. When finally alone, Rāma can reflect upon the beauty of his beloved, but again, his musings likewise are highly noble. He does not reflect on

Sītā's physical beauty, but her noble character instead, chastising himself for comparing her with the vile moon.

> *prācī disi sasi uyaū suhāvā, siya mukha sarisa dekhi sukhu pāvā* ।
> *bahuri bicāru kīnha mana māhīṁ, sīya badana sama himakara nāhīṁ* ॥

The moon rose at the Eastern horizon, which pleased him, seeing similarities with Sītā's face, he became happy. But then, he thought by himself, the moon is not like Sītā's face. — *RCM*, 1:237.5-6

> *janamu siṁdhu puni baṁdhu biēu, dina malīna sakalaṁka* ।
> *siya mukha samatā pāva kimi, caṁdu bāpuro raṁka* ॥
> — *RCM*, 1:237.7-8 and *dohā*

Its birth is from the ocean, its kinsman is poison, in the day it's weak, it has spots — how could it be compared to Sītā's face, this poor weak moon.

> *ghaṭaī baḍhai birahini dukhadāī, grasaī rāhu nija saṁdhihiṁ pāī* ।
> *koka sokaprada paṁkaja drohī, avaguna bahuta caṁdramā tohī* ।
> *baidehī mukha paṭatara dīnhe, hoi doṣu baḍa anucita kīnhe* ॥

It wanes and waxes, it brings sadness to separated lovers, Rāhu grabs it when he finds it nearby. It brings sorrow to cuckoos, it's the enemy of lotuses. O moon, you have many flaws. By comparing Videha's princess's face to the moon, I've made a totally inappropriate mistake. — *RCM*, 1:238.1-3

At this point, again, Rāma goes to his *guru* (*RCM*, 1:238.4-5) to massage his feet. In other words, the whole scene of Rāma's romantic musings is properly sandwiched in between proper *guru-sevā*.

In short, Tulsī has made it abundantly clear that both Rāma and Sītā were in the garden with proper permission of their elders and in a religious context. They met totally innocently, without prior intent. In addition, the experience of falling in love itself is totally devoid of erotic characteristics, mutual feelings are kept in strict control by the heroes themselves. Strictly speaking, there is not even a question of 'new' love, since this love is in fact an 'old' one, dating from previous births. Moreover, it is also duly sanctioned by the proper mother- and father-figures. It is entirely clear then that, whatever his inspiration, Tulsī set up his scene in a conscious contrast to Kṛṣṇa *bhakti*, by purging the erotics with a good dose of *maryādā*. Tulsī has transformed the lush Braj-scape into an urban, domesticated and controlled environment. It is no coincidence that the setting is not a wild forest bower (*kuñja*), but a nicely organised and irrigated flower garden, controlled by gardeners at every step. Tulsī's motive for this move is a religious one: he is promoting a *bhakti* of *maryādā*, fit for his *iṣṭadevatā* Rāma, often called *maryādā puruṣa*. As usual, Tulsī is engaged in theological bridge-building (term of Hawley 1989: 151): marrying the appeal of vernacular Kṛṣṇa *bhakti* with the serious serenity more befitting *bhakti* for Rāma.

Sagar's Text

What happens when this episode from Tulsī's text with *bhakti* agenda is adapted in a contemporary context? In order to answer that question I propose to analyse closely the *phulvārī* episode of Ramanand Sagar's immensely popular TV epic *Rāmāyaṇa* (video cassette vol. 2, episode 6). Given its popularity, I am assuming that this *Rāmāyaṇa*, 'hits a nerve' and reflects contemporary ideals.[6] A comparison with Tulsī's episode is all the more useful, since the director, notwithstanding his claim to take into account many regional *Rāmāyaṇas*, has made extensive use of the *Mānas* (Dalmia-Lüderitz 1991: 209), especially in this scene.

At first view, indeed, the *phulvārī* episode of the TV version seems to consist of mostly sung extracts from *Rāmcaritmānas* (or seemingly from it), interspersed with some minimal Hindī dialogue. Mainly the songs are enacted and presented as a video-clip, or rather a series of tableaux *Rāmalīlā* style.

First, before the recitation starts, but while the introductory music is playing, a procession of Sītā and her girlfriends traversing the garden on its way to the Pārvatī temple is shown. The girls enter the temple and get ready for *bhajan* singing and *pūjā,* while the camera zooms in on the image of the goddess. Then the recitation starts with a *dohā* from Tulsī's epic (*RCM,* 1:232), which describes how Rāma and Lakṣmaṇa appear from the bushes, and appropriately the two brothers are shown to enter the garden. After some lines of dialogue in which the brothers ask the gardeners for permission to pick flowers, the action shifts back to the girls in the nearby temple with equally minimal dialogue. The report of the 'adventurous' girl from Sītā's retinue upon seeing the boys is sung into a pseudo-Avadhī verse.

> *bāga bilokana rājakuṁvara dou āe* ।
> *e sakhī unake atula rūpa kī sobhā kahiyo na jāe* ॥
> — Mizokami 1992: 86

---

6. For a general evaluation of the TV series, and situating it in its performative context, as well as the media in general, see Lutgendorf 1995.

Sītā is shown to be very reluctantly dragged along while Tulsī's lines about the friends showing her the two princes from the cover of the bushes hover in the background (*RCM*, 1:232.3). From now on, no more mundane Hindī is spoken. In contrast to what is the case in *RCM*, Sagar first shows Sītā beholding Rāma, who is quite unaware of this attention. Meanwhile *RCM* is recited in the background. The first quote expresses Sītā's confused inner feelings and her inkling about this being foretold by Nārada (*sumiri sīya nārada vacana, upajī prīti punīta, cakita bilokati sakala disi, janu sisu mṛgī sabhīta*, *RCM*, 1:229 *dohā*, translated above). Interestingly, while the singer chants *prīti punīta*, 'sacred love', Sagar offers his audience a glimpse of the divine couple Viṣṇu and Lakṣmī, thus commenting, so to speak in images, on the text recited. On the other hand, while the next part of the verse describes Sītā as fearfully looking in all directions (a 'remnant' of the different sequence in Tulsī's text, where the verse occurred before she spotted the men), the camera belies this by showing a happy Sītā, steadily glancing at one object only, Rāma. Clearly, the only reason for quoting this particular *dohā* lies in the first line.

Sagar has thus established the *maryādā* context of this act, by turning the 'new love' into an old, eternal, and divine one. Next follows Tulsī's verse on Sītā's eagerness to behold Rāma more, yet stressing that it seems to her she's seeing a recovered treasure (*dekhi rūpa locana lalacāne, harașe janu nija nidhi pahicāne*, *RCM*, 1:232.4, translated above). Meanwhile, Rāma himself has looked up and is answering Sītā's glance with one of his own. Lakṣmaṇa has conveniently left the scene just a few minutes before, so as to leave Rāma and Sītā in total privacy. The camera freezes on Rāma and Sītā gazing at each other against the background of pseudo-*Mānas* singing:

> *ika dūje ko nirakhata mana na aghāe* ।
> *rāma siyā maya, siyā rāma maya, eka hī rūpa lakhāe* ॥

> Their hearts can't get enough of beholding each other. Rāma engrossed in Sītā, Sītā engrossed in Rāma. They show one single form. — Mizokami 1992: 87

This verse is sung over and over, quite elaborately. Meanwhile, the camera keeps zooming in on Rāma and Sītā respectively. Lakṣmaṇa is shown to return and look in amazement at his brother and then at Sātā. Like Lakṣmaṇa, the audience is mainly intent on watching the divine pair watching; they have become one form indeed, as the object of our and Lakṣmaṇa's glance. Next is recited, appropriately, the *Mānas caupāī* comparing them to the *cakora* bird and the moon (1:232.6), and then Sītā closes her eyes, on cue from the equivalent line from *Mānas* (*RCM*, 1:232.7). This apparent getting into a trance causes Sītā's friends to interfere and 'wake her up', but Lakṣmaṇa understands how it expresses the purity of her love and pays obeisance with a little devout bow. The girlfriends then lead Sītā away, while again the appropriate *dohā* about Sītā turning back again and again is sung (*RCM*, 1:232 *dohā*).

The scene in the Pārvatī temple is then enacted, while a shortened version of Sītā's prayer from *RCM* is sung (1:236.5-6 and 237.2-4a). These are the lines where Sītā says she won't ask for anything explicitly because the all-knowing goddess is sure to know her heart's desire anyway. Tulsī's lines follow, describing how pleased the goddess is with Sītā's humble devotion (*RCM*, 1:237.5a). While the rest of Tulsī's text is recited (*RCM*, 1:237.5b-6), the miraculous shedding of the garland is enacted. Finally, Pārvatī's blessing granting Sītā's wishes (*RCM*, 1:237.7-8 and the *chanda*) is sung, not in chorus but by one single voice, as if the exact words from the image's lips. While the *chanda* ends, Sītā exits.

Finally, this episode of the TV *Rāmāyaṇa* is wound up with two parallel scenes. In one Rāma is shown musing about the similarity of the moon to Sītā's face in Lakṣmaṇa's company, with some dialogue, to which we will come back, and quotes from *RCM*, 1:237.7-8 and *dohā*. The camera then shifts back once again to Sītā's girlfriends, who similarly compare Rāma's face to the moon. Sītā is portrayed as lost in dreams, she does not say a word. This last scene has no equivalent in *RCM*, and hence there are no quotes in the background. The episode ends when one of the girlfriends voices doubt that such a delicate prince as Rāma would be able to lift the bow, which fore-shadows the next episode.

Superficially then, the TV episode appears to follow Tulsī very closely and may not seem to warrant much further comparison.

However, upon closer investigation, some interesting shifts in focus can be detected, by studying closely what Sagar chooses to preserve of *RCM*, what he discards, and where he innovates.

For one, the whole Flower Garden scene is viewed mainly from Sītā's perspective: most quotes from *RCM* are verses to that effect. Rāma's musings about his feelings to his brother are simply skipped, at least for the time being (till the next scene makes them explicit). Rāma hardly loses his composure, the way Tulsī had suggested. He keeps sporting an all-knowing smile on his face throughout.

If Rāma's feelings are hardly touched upon during the scene proper, it is Sītā's reaction that is important. Whereas in Tulsī's text, Rāma spotted the women first, Sagar has Sītā and her friends spying on a completely unaware Rāma. The result is that the audience identifies with Sītā's perspective. This stress on the devotee rather than on the object of veneration is most obvious from the fact that Sagar leaves out the whole *nakha-śikha* description of the brothers. This omission may have to do also with the conventions of the medium he is using. Sagar is after all a Bollywood movie director, and in the popular film, the camera lingers on the woman's body, rather than the man's. However, we do not see a full reversal to erotic descriptions of Sītā's beauty either, as we had seen in the *kāvya* texts. Nor does the camera end up voyeuristically lingering on Sītā's physical beauty. Camera movement remains well 'above the belt' and is mainly concentrating on Sītā's eyes meeting Rāma's. Sagar may be working in a secular genre, but he keeps his 'text' free from eroticism.

The gaze of Sagar's camera then is, as in Tulsī's text, directed to the gazing of the protagonists themselves, to their mutual *darśana* (the stress on *darśana*, which fits well with traditional theatrical convention, has been noted for the epic as a whole (see Lutgendorf 1995: 230-31). This is also apparent in the reactions of the other characters: the girfriends stare at Sītā, Lakṣmaṇa gazes at Rāma gazing at Sītā. The secondary characters are portrayed as interested in their brother or friend's 'falling in love' rather than in the other sex *per se*. Clearly, the audience is invited to identify with them rather than with Rāma, or even Sītā. This is well-illustrated by the 'made-up' Avadhī verse that is repeated over and over again while Sītā and Rāma behold. It goes quite a bit further in theological interpretation than the *Mānas* itself, as it suggests a unity between Rāma and Sītā. As the divine pair melts together, it is the audience beholding the pair, rather than the pair beholding each other that takes centre stage.

What we said earlier about the absence of Rāma's perspective needs to be modified in the light of the romantic scene following the Flower Garden scene. Here, while the brothers are gazing at the moon, the issue of Rāma's reaction is addressed. On the one hand, Sagar did not want his 'beholding' scene interrupted by it, but apparently he did consider the matter far too important to be left in Avadhī, the point of which might conceivably escape his audience. As in Tulsī's text, Rāma confesses his unusual feelings to his brother, but after the Flower Garden scene proper. The same business of the inappropriateness of a Rāghava gazing upon 'strange women' is raised. In Sagar's version, Lakṣmaṇa takes the clue, which was only hinted at in Tulsī's and states that may be Sītā is destined to be Rāma's wife. Rāma answers that only god knows, an ironic statement, since the audience is of course very well aware that Rāma is in the end God himself. This scene seems to be designed according to the commentatorial tradition of countering objections (*śaṅkā-samādhāna*), here with regard to the possiblity of inappropriate behaviour of Rāma (for the tradition, see Lutgendorf 1991a: 393). Indeed, as we shall see, that is clearly a major concern of Sagar's.

It also pays off to look closely at the careful selection Sagar has made from the about eight *kaḍavak*s that constitute the Flower Garden episode proper. He has in effect concentrated mainly on two passages from Tulsī's text, namely *kaḍavak*s 232 and 236-37, and added only one *dohā* from 229. His selection is partly driven by narrative concerns (the verses describe 'the action', such as there is), but also reveals agenda which is especially clear from the 'exceptional' quote from 229. This *dohā* is about the purity of Sītā's love as in accordance with Nārada's prediction. As we have seen, this *dohā* is taken out of context and its second line does not fit what Sagar's camera shows. Clearly, it is the first line, with its legitimising aspect that is its *raison d'être*. Clearly, Sagar has been attracted especially to the passages where Tulsī stresses the legitimacy of the meeting of the hero and the heroine: the rest of the quotes stress Sītā's shyness and her bashfully closing her eyes. Most importantly, he chooses to show completely the scene where Sītā receives the blessing of Pārvatī, the divine mother, for her choice of groom.

Sagar has provided even more justification for the legitimacy of the young people being in the garden. Before the Flower Garden episode proper, Rāma and Lakṣmaṇa were shown taking leave from their *guru,* and getting proper permission to go and pick flowers for the *pūjā.* In Sagar's version, it is Viśvāmitra himself who directs the boys to go to the garden near the palace's Gaurīmandir (Mizokami 1992: 86). Here, Sāgar is satisfying a possible objection (*śaṅkā-samādhāna*) one might have come up with, were one inclined to doubt the purity of Rāma's motives. In Sagar's version, the princes are present in that very flower garden because their *guru* had ordained such, and one might speculate, the *guru* in his omniscience, is foreseeing what will happen. Even more blessing from the elders, if needed.

Just before that, Sagar had introduced another innovation in the same vein. Sītā is shown to be sent by her mother to the garden for worshiping Pārvatī. This is portrayed as directly connected with the *svayaṁvara* which is to take place the next day. Sītā and her girlfriends receive the plates with worship materials from their elders, and they even ask whether some older lady should accompany them as chaperone (*āp bhī calkar pūjān karāie na kākī jī,* Mizokami 1992: 85). However, the answer they receive is that worship of Pārvatī as virgin, or *kumārī,* is only done by virgins (*kuṁvārī kanyā*). No such stress on the virginal status of the goddess or her devotees comes up in Tulsī's text. It seems that Sagar has gone out of his way to ensure a proper *maryādā* atmosphere. What he is doing in this extra scene is countering yet another possible objection (*śaṅkā-samādhāna*) one might have come up with, were one inclined to doubt the purity of Sītā's motives. She did not on her own account venture out without an elder chaperone. Even the absence of elder is ascribed to the command of elders.

If we add to the study of the selections of *RCM* and the innovation of the introduction scenes, also the concluding scene described earlier, which affirms that Rāma's love for Sītā is of the *svakīyā* type, it is abundantly clear that Sagar was interested in situating this blossoming of love within the boundaries of *maryādā*. He says as much explicitly during a sermon at the conclusion of volume 3 of the video series, while commenting on the later occasion of the *svayaṁvara* scene (Dalmia-Lüderitz 1991: 224-25).

Of course, he is not the first commentator to stress these matters. One of the famous commentators, Ramkinkar Upadhyay, stresses the same point. He speaks explicitly about this episode to be studded in *maryādā* like a jewel in gold (Upadhyay 1974, 1: 288), and calls Tulsī's treatment of this scene of prenuptial love a golden mid-way between too much stress on either duty or love (p. 189). The commentator by whom Sagar reportedly was influenced, Morārī Bāpū (Lutgendorf 1995: 228), similarly stresses the *maryādā* aspects of the scene. He makes a big deal out of *maryādā-puruṣa* Rāma's insisting on asking permission to pick the flowers from the gardeners, though Laksmaṇa finds it natural that, as guests of the king, they would just go ahead (Bāpū 1986: 239). Further, he stresses that Rāma and Sītā meet in the morning, not in the evening, as young people nowadays do to the dismay of their parents (p. 240). Hereby the commentator has clearly linked the scene to modern-day dating concerns and set up Rāma and Sītā as a model for young pre-maritally dating couples. Morārī Bāpū also gives a 'spiritual' interpretation of the scene, which is in line with the treatment of Sītā as metaphor for the *bhakta*. He even assigns the 'bold' *sakhī* the role of the *guru*, since she is the one who will give Sītā *darśana* of Rāma, and

Lakṣmaṇa becomes the *pūjārī*, who dresses Rāma up for *darśana* (pp. 241-42). (Note that Bāpū sticks to Tulsī's scenario where Rāma first sees his devotee, before the devotee spots him.) And of course he makes much out of Sītā closing her eyes, as if she wanted to stick with the spritual and had no more need for the rest of the world (pp. 242-43). Finally, Bāpū also stresses *maryādā* elements such as the blessing of the goddess, and both Sītā's and Rāma's immediate confession of what happened to their elders (p. 245).

If Sagar then clearly shared Tulsī's and traditional commentators' concern to stress *maryādā*, the question is what was his motive. One may well doubt whether the film director's agenda was equally theological as Tulsī's. After all, Sagar is not working in a context where erotic Kṛṣṇa *bhakti* is predominant and needed to be downplayed in favour of more serene and stern Rāma *bhakti*. Rather, Sagar's universe of operating is a different one, and a profoundly secular one.

Sagar, as a popular movie director, is working against the backdrop of the 'eroticism' of the Bollywood cinema genre. In fact, the whole scene fits well within the cliches of the genre, in the sense that the action is halted to have the emotions of hero and heroine marked with a song and dance sequence. Usually, such scenes are set in bucolic environs, in the outdoors, and the flower garden setting fits well in that sense.

However, in contrast to the Bollywood movie, we don't have a hip-gyrating heroine. Sītā does not venture to dance. Rather, the Pārvatī *pūjā* scene is reminiscent of such devotional movies as *Jai Santoshi Ma*. Sagar is following the lines of the divide between the so-called 'mythological' movie and the 'social' one. In doing so, he marks his product as distanced from commercial voyeurism. In contrast to the couples of the popular cinema, which could be said to represent a dream of teenagers, Sītā and Rāma model a love that can be approved of in religious terms, which incorporates at the same time the dream of the teenager and the ideal of the parent/elder.

Interestingly, such differences are also marked by language. Whereas the average Bollywood movie uses a standard spoken Hindī with a fair sprinkling of colloquialisms and some 'romantic' Urdu vocabulary, Sagar's characters speak all High Hindī, in a very Sanskritic style. Interestingly, the whole point of Tulsī's *RCM* had been to 'vernacularise' the Sanskrit, whereas in Sāgar's work we see the linguistic ṛegister swing exactly the other way. This fits, however, well with the way Tulsī's work is used today: increasingly, it is being ritualised, used more for connotation than content, a process which has been noticed and marked as 'Sanskritisation' by Lutgendorf (1991a: 56-96, and 1991b).

Sagar is also working against the background of the secular Soap series on Durdarshan, or DD. His *Rāmāyaṇa* indeed started out as a 'soap opera of the gods' (*Sunday* as quoted in Mitra 1993: 85), designed to be a mythological counterpart to the successful secular series such as Ramesh Sippy's *Buniyād* and Kumar Vasudev's *Hum Log*. Such soaps had functioned as a mix between 'didactic' and 'entertainment' programmes on DD since the eighties (Mitra 1993: 36-38 and 78-89). Their main function seems to have been to address middle-class family concerns against a backdrop of national integration (Mitra 1993: 99). One of the social issues given air time in such series is that of marriage, in particular the issue of the legitimacy of the love marriage as compared to the more traditional arranged marriage.

When viewed in this context, Sagar's concern for *maryādā* takes on different dimensions than that of Tulsī's theology. It seems obvious that Sagar is engaged in situating romance within *maryādā*, in sending the message to the younger generation that pre-nuptial meetings are okay only when strictly controlled by *maryādā* factors. This message, that love and *dharma* must be made to cohere, rather than conflict is of course not new to Sagar. It is in conformity with what has been noted to be one of the central imperatives of the Hindi movie, the heart (*dil*) is valued and a *sine qua non* for the hero, but needs to be brought into harmony with duty and principles (*kartavya, usūl*) (see Thomas 1995).

A Popular Movie: *Hum Aap Ke Hain Koun*

Finally, I'd like to turn to the third text under investigation, the popular 1994 hit-movie *Hum aap ke hain koun*, 'What am I to you?', directed by Sooraj R. Barjatya. This movie has been a trend-setter and has inaugurated a wave of family entertainment type of films that has since continued, so arguably it is an important cinema landmark to investigate contemporary audience concerns.

Even though this movie is not a 'mythological', there are several very explicit references to *Rāmāyaṇa* in general and *RCM* in particular. Of course, references to mythological themes, especially the *Rāmāyaṇa*, in popular movies are nothing new or unusual (for some speculations regarding the market forces underlying the inclusion of mythological features in the mix of ingredients of the Hindi movie, see, e.g., Derné 1995b). However, if we get beyond merely identifying 'timeless' mythological models underlying a particular Hindi movie, into studying how exactly they are used, and which selection has been made in the process, we stand to learn a great deal about the reception of the models at a given moment. This gives us an interesting insight in how the messages from *Rāmāyaṇa* spill over in a secular context in the mid-nineties.

Let us first look at how the general *Rāmāyaṇa* mythology is used to frame the story. Importantly, Rāma is the family deity or *kula-devatā* in the house of the heroes of this movie, and is worshipped in several scenes throughout the movie. The heroes themselves are an elder brother, named Rajesh (Mohnish Behl), and his younger brother, Prem (Salman Khan). Rajesh, befitting the elder brother role, is the stern one, and functions as a *maryādā-puruṣa,* or a Rāma type. Prem, on the other hand, is not a Lakṣmaṇa type. His name may be a clue to the fact that the director sees in him a Kṛṣṇa-like character.[7] And this is confirmed by his actions, notably his flirting with and charming all the women and inventing a good many tricks. But notwithstanding this countercurrent, the heroes' household is clearly one in which Rāma's *maryādā* prevails.

Conforming to Bollywood conventions, Rajesh and Prem are orphans who have been raised by their bachelor uncle (*kākā*) Kailāśnāth, their late father's younger brother. He has the responsibility of arranging Rajesh's wedding, and has prospected a bride, in the form of his old school friend's daughter, Pūjā (Renuka Shahne). However, in order to ensure Rajesh's personal happiness, he seeks to arrange for him a pre-marital meeting with his future bride so that the future pair has a chance to get to know each other before the big step. Rajesh is not aware of the plot being arranged for him, and lured along on the pretext of a pilgrimage trip to Rāmṭek, where Pūjā happens to be holidaying with her family. Like Rāma and Sītā of Tulsī's and the TV version, Rajesh and Pujā's

---

7. This is confirmed in as many words in the movie during the traditional 'goodbye' song at the 'farewell-ceremony' (*bidā*) for the bride at the end of the wedding, where the words are: 'your father-in-law is like a father, your husband like a god, your brother-in-law is a spitting-image of Kṛṣṇa' (*sasurjī pitā hai, pati devatā hai, devar chabi kṛṣṇa kī*). The camera zooms in on Prem at this point.

pre-marital meeting is in no way a rendezvous set-up by the boy or girl themselves.

Significantly, the setting of the first meeting between Rajesh and Pūjā is Rāmṭek, a shrine devoted to Rāma. In the movie it is a beautiful modern Hindu temple complex, with the familiar marble *mūrti* of Rāma flanked by Lakṣmaṇa and Sītā in the main shrine. When the camera catches its first glimpse of the temple complex, *Mānas* recitation is heard in the background, to set the proper devotional atmosphere.[8] Several other explicit references to *Rāmcaritmānas* ensue. Most notably, this occurs when Pūjā and her father, Siddhārtha, are experimenting in the kitchen of their room and break a pot. So as to escape the wrath of his wife, Siddhārtha quickly pretends he was all along reciting from the *Mānas*, and appropriately chooses the episode where Rāma breaks Śiva's bow. His wife sees through the device, but Siddhārtha cleverly casts her in the role of the quickly angered Paraśurāma, and himself in that of the patient and all-enduring Rāma. Such playful appropriation of the Rāma-story presumes on the part of the viewer a more than superficial awareness of the mythology. It clearly suggests that the film-maker quite emphatically wants to frame his story within a traditional context, guided by models from *Rāmāyaṇa*, and in particular Tulsīdās's version of the story.

As could be expected, given the essential love-story content of this 'social' movie, it is in particular the model of Rāma and Sītā falling in love that looms large in the background. The love story of Rajesh and Pūjā gets off to a

---

8. The verses recited are 7.90 *dohā* 'k': *binu viśvāsa bhagati nahīṁ tehi binu dravahi na rāma, rāma kṛpā binā sapanehū jīva na laha viśrāma* (Without faith there is no devotion, without it Rāma does not 'melt', without Rāma's grace, even in a dream, a human soul cannot reach peace) and 1:112.*caupāī* 4: *maṁgala bhavana amaṁgalahārī, dravaū ju dasaratha ajira bihārī* (Abode of auspiciousness, remover of inauspiciousness, playful child in Daśaratha's courtyard, have mercy on me).

good start. The match for Rajesh is an arranged one, but during the holiday both parties acually fall in love. Their 'courting' proceeds quite *maryādā*-like, with lots of scope for sweetly shy bashfulness on behalf of Pūjā and controlled yet growing interest on the part of Rajesh. Several elements of the scene where the couple meets the first time are reminiscent of Rāma and Sītā's first meeting as shown in Sagar's TV version. Pūjā and her sister look at the brothers from behind the kitchen doors like Sītā and her girlfriends from behind the bushes. When called upon to appear before her future fiance, Pūjā first hesitates, and has to be pushed ahead by her sister. Rajesh is equally modest. The scene immediately following the first meeting is reminiscent of the one with the moon-gazing brothers in the TV *Rāmāyaṇa*. Prem is massaging his elder brother's legs, an ideal moment for confidances. He has to ask Rajesh quite explicitly whether he liked the girl he met or not, and Rajesh does not even answer, he just smiles. Upon which Prem draws his own conclusions, congratulates his astonished brother, and spreads the news. Clearly, the protagonists are equally inhibited as Sītā and Rāma and it is their brother and sister-confidante who are actively promoting the pair's moments of togetherness and who encourage and voice the feelings of their siblings. Major differences are there too, of course, especially in the form of the presence of the elders (which is more like *Mahāvīracaritra* than like *Mānas*). However, that confirms only the similarity of the major message, which is that love flourishes within *maryādā* boundaries.

This message is well epitomised in the song *vāh vāh rāmajī* congratulations Rāmajī' that accompanies the engagement celebrations. Just the first few lines, part of which function as refrain, say it all:

vāh vāh rāmajī, joḍī kyā banāī
bhaiyyā aur bhābhī ko, badhāī ho badhāī
sab rasmoṁ se baḍī hai jismeṁ dil se dil kī sagāī

> Well-done, Rāmajī, what a match have you made [in heaven]. To my brother and sister-in-law, congratulations, congratulations. The best of all ceremonies/traditions, is the one in which hearts get engaged.

It could hardly be more explicitly put: wedding traditional values (*maryādā*) with love is the theme the film-maker wants to promote with the movie. At the same time, these categories seem to be connected to tradition and modernity, and to some extent with East and West. The ceremony itself is a wonderful blend of Western influence, the rings that are exchanged, and Hindu customs and setting (in the temple of course, with rites such as the feeding of the groom-to-be, lighting of a *diyā* and setting it afloat in the temple tank and other *pūjā* rituals).

After these initial tone-setting scenes with explicit *Mānas* references, the movie continues to develop the same message. The wedding festivities, with their jocular abandon, take place appropriately in the house of the bride, where Kṛṣṇa is the presiding deity. However, after the wedding, Rāma again prevails. When Pūjā enters her *sasurāla* or 'in-laws'-house' she is presented with a copy of *Rāmāyaṇa* as a wedding-gift (from her husband's maternal uncle or *māmā*), who says superfluously: 'This is the *Rāmāyaṇa*, daughter-in-law, Sītā is daughter-in-law in there' (*rāmāyaṇa hai bahū, ismeṁ sītā hai bahū*). More than once, Pūjā is shown to perform worship of the *kula-devatā*, Rāma, and she expresses her faith in him at several significant turns of the story (such as when the servant Lallū is anguishing about a sick family member and she comforts him by giving him *prasāda* from the image and voicing strong faith that everything will turn out right in the end).

Pūjā's *sasurāla* or 'in-laws-house' is portrayed as a paradise where *maryādā* and love are in perfect harmony, presided over by *kula-devatā* Rāma. Potential tensions between *sasurāla* and *māyakā* are downplayed by the familiar device of the absence of real parents-in-law, and the fact that Rajesh's uncle is an old friend of the father of the bride. In case we missed the message about what this movie is all about, we just need to read what is written large on our 'rebel' Prem's fancy car: 'I love my family'. *Maryādā* and family values with a happy face of plenty and scope for the occasional harmless prank.

Rajesh and Pūjā's ideal Rāma-and-Sītā-like wedding has its counterpart in the blossoming love between Prem and Pūjā's sister, Niśā (Madhuri Dixit). This pair is much more of the Kṛṣṇa and Rādhā type. Befitting a girl for prankster Prem, Niśā holds her ground in the boisterous repartees and seems to have snappy replies ready for all occasions. Of course, Madhuri's character engages liberally in non-Sītā-esque gyrating hip-swinging, yet there are significant *maryādā*-markers in this relationship too. Most of the dance scenes are in fact cast as part of such family-affirming celebrations as engagement, wedding, and birth of Pūjā and Rajesh's son. True to the Bollywood stratagems, the culmination of Prem and Niśā's love is enacted in the usual Bollywood escapist 'pseudo-folk harvesting scene' (with the song: *yah mausam hai jādū kā mitvā*). However, and here it gets particularly interesting for our purpose, in addition, this love also receives divine sanction.

After their rural excursion, Prem and Niśā are shown to drop by again in the very same Rāmṭek temple where their brother and sister's engagement was celebrated. During their visit, while Prem half-jokingly pays his respects to the manager, Niśā prepares a *diyā* to be lit and set afloat in the temple pond, just as her sister did for her engagement. What is recited in the background, is precisely the scene from *RCM* where Sītā gets sanction in the temple by Pārvatī.

> *mora manorathu jānahu nīkeṁ, basahu sadā ura pura sabahī keṁ* ।
> *kīnheuṁ pragaṭa na kārana tehīṁ, asa kahi carana gahe baidehīṁ* ॥

> 'You know my wish well, you dwell always in everyone's heart. For that reason I have not expressed it.' Praying thus, Vaidehī grasped [Pārvatī's] feet.
>
> — *RCM*, 1:2362-3

> *binaya prema basa bhī bhavānī, khasī māla mūrati musukānī* ।
> *sādara siyaṁ prasādu sira dhareū, bolī gauri haraṣu hiyaṁ bhareū* ॥

> The Goddess, impressed by [Sītā's] humility and love, smilingly shed a garland from her image. Sītā respectfully placed this 'materialised grace' (*prasāda*) on her head, and Gaurī spoke, her heart filled with joy.

This passage catches the end of Sītā's prayer, where she modestly refrains from naming the man whom she desires for husband, namely Rāma, whom she has just met in the flower garden. As we have seen, the goddess is portrayed as impressed both by Sītā's love and her humility. It is no coincidence that these lines are the very ones quoted in Sagar's TV series. We see here a trend developing. It is not just a particular scene from Tulsī's work that becomes popular. There is a concept of love that goes with it. Clearly, *maryādā* is seen as a necessary compliment of love. The script writer has done a great job in picking those two *caupāī* lines from the *RCM*!

At this point, Prem asks Niśā why she is lighting the *diyā*, at which Niśā truthfully answers that her mother had told her to do so, as indeed, she had before Niśā and Prem set out on their trip. Here we have yet another parallel to Sītā, whose presence in the garden was justified by her mother's command to perform *pūjā* of Pārvatī. Again, this is something that, as we have seen, was picked up on and explicitly portrayed by Sagar in his TV *Rāmāyaṇa* (vol. 2, episode 6). In short, the seemingly *masālā* heroine Niśā has received a double blessing, one maternal, one divine, and this with quite explicit reference to the model of Sītā. In general, the scene nicely sets the tone for the romance of Niśā and Prem, which progresses in a convincingly non-Platonic way and with Bollywood *masālā*, but always within bounds of happy, playful *maryādā*. Rāma presides even over this relationship.

Most interesting for our purpose is how the mythological model gets linked up with contemporary concerns. Quite clearly the message to young people is that the ideal which renders a maximum amount of happiness is a love-marriage that proceeds with the parents' blessing and preferably even coincides with the match arranged by them. Modernity and Hindu tradition don't need to be in conflict, compromise is just around the corner, with a bit of patience, obedience, and clever helping out by fate.

This is exemplified further in the story when uncle Kailāśnāth has put the matter of Prem's marriage in the hands of Pūjā. Pūjā then asks Prem whether he prefers 'love marriage' or 'arranged marriage'. His reply is: *Bhābhī, 'love marriage' jo āp ko arranged karā di hai* 'A love marriage that has been arranged for you'. Significantly, even the language is a mix of Hindī and English, and the answer proposes a hip blend of tradition and modernity. None of our youngsters is going to miss the point: some initiative is fine, but these matters are not to be discussed openly with elders! Enlisting of siblings' help though is permitted. Needless to say Pūjā is delighted when she finds out that Prem's chosen bride is her very own sister, Niśā. If the movie had ended there, already the message would be clear. However, the love of Prem and Nishā still stands to be substantially tested. This 'trial by fire' has its own mythological resonances, which deserve more elaborate attention than I can give within the scope of this paper, and plan to discuss elsewhere. In any case, as regards pre-marital love, there is no doubt about the movie-maker's solution. Love-within-*maryādā* is writ large all over the place, if not actually on Prem's car.

Conclusion

We have traced the portrayal of the episode of Rāma and Sītā's first love in Tulsīdās's medieval text, through Sagar's late-eighties TV version, to a contemporary popular hit movie. In all these versions, we found a clear concern with embedding love within the bounds of *maryādā,* or conventional morality. Tulsī's agenda was a theological one: promoting devotion for *maryādā-puruṣa* Rāma, possibly countering the erotic tone of the Kṛṣṇa *bhakti* counterpart. In the contemporary TV and film versions we find a strong social concern with the role-model value of the divine pair. The way their love develops as a happy 'wedding' of 'love' and 'arranged' marriage is portrayed as exemplary. If anything, the *maryādā* factor is stressed even stronger than in Tulsī's version. In the popular Bollywood portrayal we end up with an interesting *khicaḍī* of modernity and tradition, which we might well describe as *masālā-maryādā.*

Abbreviations

C : ***Cāndāyana:*** *Dāud viracit pratham Hindī sūfī prem-kāvya.*

MC : *Mahākaviśrībhavabhūtipraṇītaṁ* ***Mahāvīracaritaṁ*** *vīrarāghavakṛtayā bhāvapradyotinīvyākhyayā samalaṁkṛtam.*

P : *Jāyasī Granthāvalī arthāt* ***Padmāvat****, Akharāvaṭ aur Ākharī kalām.*

PR : *Mahākavijayadevaviracitam* ***Prasannarāghavam****.*

RCM : *Śrīmadgosvāmī Tulsīdāsjīviracita* ***Śrīrāmcaritmānas****.*

Bibliography

PRIMARY SOURCES

Bāpū, Morārī, *Rāmcaritmānas-kathā*, Bombay: Prācīn Saṁskṛti Mandir, 1986.

Grimal, François. ed. and tr., *Mahākaviśrībhavabhūtipraṇītaṁ Mahāvīracaritaṁ vīrarāghavakṛtayā bhāvapradyotinīvyākhyayā samalaṁkṛtam (Le Mahāvīracarita de Bhavabhūti accompagné du commentaire de Vīrarāghava).* Publications de l'institut Français d'Indologie 74. Pondichéry: Institut Francais, 1989.

Gupta, Mātāprasād, *Cāndāyana: Dāud viracit praham Hindī sūfī prem-kāvya.* Vārāṇasī: Viśvavidyālay Prakāśan, 1967.

Mizokami, Tomio, ed., *Ramayana: A TV serial by Ramanand Sagar*, Osaka: Osaka University of Foreign Studies, 1992.

Poddār, Hanumānprasād, ed. and comm., *Śrīmadgosvāmī Tulsīdāsjī viracita Śrīrāmcaritmānas*, Gorakhpur: Gītā Press [1942] 1990.

Sagar, Ramanand, *Rāmāyaṇa*, Video cassettes, 1987.

Śaran, Anjaninandan, ed. and comm, *Mānas pīyūē*, 12 vols., Ayodhya: Mānas Pīyuē Karyālay, 1925-56.

Śāstrī, Rāmnāth Tripāṭhī and Ramākānt Tripāṭhī, eds. and comms., *Mahākavijayadevaviracitaṁ Prasannarāghavam (Vibhā Saṁskṛta-Hindī vyākhyopetam)*, Vārāṇasī: Caukhambā Amarbhārtī Prakāśan, 1977.

Śukla, Ācārya Rāmcandra, ed., *Jāyasī Granthāvalī arthāt Padmāvat, Akharāvaṭ aur Ākharī kalām*, Nāgarīpracāriṇī Granthmālā 31, Vārāṇasī: Nāgarīpracāriṇī Sabhā, 1995 [1924].

Upadhyay, Ramkinkar, *Mānas-muktāvalī*, Calcutta: Biralā Academy of Art and Culture, 1974.

SECONDARY SOURCES

Breckenridge, Carol E., ed., *Consuming modernity: Public culture in a South Asian world*, Minneapolis: University of Minnesota Press, 1995.

Dalmia-Lüderitz, Vasudha, 'Television and tradition: Some observations on the serialization of the Rāmāyaṇa', In: Monika Thiel-Horstmann, ed., *Rāmāyaṇa and Rāmāyaṇas*, Wiesbaden: Otto Harrassowitz, 207-28, 1991.

De, Sushil Kumar, *The early history of the Vaishnava faith and movement in Bengal*, 2nd edn., Calcutta: Firma KLM. 1961.

Derné, Steve, *Culture in action: Family life, emotion, and male dominance in Banaras, India*, Albany: State University of New York Press, 1995a.

———, 'Market forces at work: Religious themes in commercial Hindi films', In: Babb, Lawrence & Susan Wadley, eds., *Media and the transformation of religion in South Asia*, 191-216, Philadelphia: University of Pennsylvania Press, 1995b.

Hawley, John Stratton, and Mark Juergensmeyer, *Songs of the Saints of India*, Oxford: Oxford University Press, 1988.

Kakar, Sudhir, *The inner world: A psycho-analythical study of childhood and society in India*, 2nd edn., Delhi: Oxford University Press, 1981.

Lutgendorf, Philip, 1991a, *The life of a text : performing the Ramcaritmanas of Tulsidas*, Berkeley: University of California Press.

———, 'The "great sacrifice" of *Rāmāyaṇa* recitation: Ritual performance of the *Rāmcaritmānas*', In: Monika Thiel-Horstmann, ed., *Rāmāyaṇa and Rāmāyaṇas*, Wiesbaden: Otto Harrassowitz, 1991b, 185-205.

———, 'The secret life of Rāmcandra of Ayodhya', In: Paula Richman, ed., *Many Ramayanas: the diversity of a narrative tradition. in South Asia*, Berkeley: University of California Press, 1994. 217-34.

———, 'All in the (Raghu) family', In: Babb, Lawrence & Susan Wadley, eds., *Media and the transformation of religion in South Asia*, 217-53, Philadelphia: University of Pennsylvania Press, 1995.

Mitra, Ananda, *Television and popular culture in India: A study of the Mahabharat*, New Delhi: Sage Publications, 1993.

Raheja, Goria Goodwin, 'Women's speech genres, kinship and contradiction', In: Nita Kumar, ed., *Women as subjects: South Asian histories*, Charlottesville: University Press of Virginia, 1994.

Shirreff, A.G., tr., *Padmāvatī*, Bibliotheca Indica 267, Calcutta: The Royal Asiatic Society of Bengal, 1944.

Shulman, David, 'Fire and flood: The testing of Sītā in Kampaṉ's Irāmāvatāram', In: Paula Richman, ed., *Many Ramayanas: the diversity of a narrative tradition, in South Asia*, Berkeley: University of California Press: 1991, 89-113.

Thomas, Rosie, 'Melodrama and the negotiation of morality in mainstream Hindi film', In: Breckenridge 1995, 157-82.

Vaudeville, Charlotte, *Etude sur les sources et la composition du Rāmāyaṇa de Tulsī-Dās*, Paris: Adrien Maisonneuve, 1955.

5

Anklets Away

The Symbolism of Jewellery and Ornamentation in Vālmīki's Rāmāyaṇa

Sally J. Sutherland Goldman

Abstract

This paper will examine how beauty — both male and female — is defined and articulated by Vālmīki in his monumental epic, the *Rāmāyaṇa*. Physical beauty is equated with ornamentation, a concept made clear in numerous passages throughout the epic. The inverse is also true in general; lack of ornamentation marks a lack of physical beauty. However, it is when there is absence of ornamentation, especially in regard to those very characters whose viability depends on their beauty, that we see the poetic genius of Vālmīki at work.

Who wears ornaments and why? Brides are adorned with jewellery, wives wear it, but widows remove their jewels and other ornamentation — women undertaking *satī*, however, ornament themselves.[1] Ornamentation of the body and the wearing of jewellery is known in the earliest extant literary

1. Alf Hiltebeitel, correctly in my opinon, aligns the wearing of jewels with auspiciousness, and a woman's status as a *sumaṅgalī* (Hiltebeitel 1981).

records we have,[2] and by the time of the epics, is pervasive. Thus, the wearing of jewellery in Vālmīki's *Rāmāyaṇa* is seemingly commonplace, but is it meaningful? The question is not original. Alf Hiltebeitel raises the issue of Draupadī's and Sītā's ornamentation, associating its significance with the two figures' connection with the Goddess [1980, 1981a, 1981b]. But his arguments are gender specific, focusing exclusively on the two epic heroines' wearing of ornaments. Sheldon Pollock makes mention of ornaments in his translations of the Ayodhyā and Araṇya Kāṇḍa [1986, 1991]. In his Introduction to the Ayodhyā Kāṇḍa, he draws our attention to the fact that 'Sītā at one point is said to be wearing jewelry, then not wearing it, then again wearing it (34.17,54.16,82.13)' [1986:25], but attributes this only to the inconsistencies and discrepencies of Vālmīki's text [1986:25]. Again in his note on *Vālmīki Rāmāyṇa* 3.49.2 [1991: 323] he questions the significance of ornamentation. Here, he comments, 'It is remarkable how frequently attention is called to the jewelry worn by *rākṣasa*s (in the Araṇya Kāṇḍa alone 24.20, 25.7, 30.9, 33.8, 36.2, 36.13, 42.16, 47.7, 57.24).' Pollock, however, fails to take the matter any further, noting only, 'What is unclear, however, is the significance we should attribute to this detail'. It is my contention that in Vālmīki's text we can see a very clear pattern emerging as to who is marked as wearing jewellery and when, and that this patterning is significant. And, I believe and hope to demonstrate, that for Vālmīki the wearing of, exchanging of, and secreting away of jewellery is a clear reference to one's status as a sexual being.

The wearing of jewellery is not specifically associated with gender, although the specific types of jewellery mentioned

---

2. For example, *Ṛgveda*, 10.125.

are not uncommonly gender specific. The *rākṣasas* to which Pollock's comment refers are male.[3] Vālmīki, however, does seem to make a connection between the wearers of ornaments, here the *rākṣasas*, and the nature of the individual wearing the ornaments. Take, for example, Vālmīki's first detailed description of the epic's major antagonist, the lord of the *rākṣasas*, Rāvaṇa. This passage is found in the third book of the epic, the Araṇya Kāṇḍa, and presents an imposing and heavily ornamented figure:

> She [Śūrpanakhā] found Rāvaṇa in his splendid palace, radiant in his power, his advisers sitting beside him like the Maruts next to Vāsava. He was seated upon a golden throne radiant as the sun, and he looked like a fire on a golden altar blazing with rich oblations. . . .[4] He had twenty arms and ten necks. His regalia was a wonder to behold. A broad-chested, mighty king, he was marked with all the marks of royalty. He sparkled with earrings of burnished gold and the glossy beryl he wore. His arms were handsome, his teeth bright white, his mouth huge, and he was as tall as a mountain. . . . The *rākṣasa* woman beheld this savage and powerful brother of hers, clad in heavenly

---

3. In fact, in Vālmīki, *rākṣasīs* are rarely mentioned as wearing ornaments, an issue that is addressed below.

4. All references are to the critical edition of the *Vālmīki Rāmāyaṇa*. All translations are taken from the Princeton translation of the *Vālmīki Rāmāyaṇa* (Robert P. Goldman, *et al.*) unless otherwise noted. The omitted verses are:

   A hero invincible in combat with gods, *gandharvas*, spirits, or great seers, he looked like Death himself with jaws agape. He carried lightning-bolt wounds received in clashes with gods and *asuras*. His chest was seamed with scars where Airāvata's pointed tusks had gored him (3.30.6-7).

garments and jewels, adorned with heavenly garlands, the illustrious lord of *rākṣasas*, delight of the House of the Paulastyas. — 3.30.4-5,8-9,1[5]

Later, in the Sundara Kāṇḍa, as Hanumān searches the demon's residence, we are given another detailed description:

> On that glittering bed, the great monkey saw the mighty lord of the *rākṣasas* sleeping. With his red eyes, great arms, garments shot with gold, and his precious dazzling earrings, he resembled a great storm cloud. His body smeared with fragrant red sandalpaste, he truly resembled a cloud laced with streaks of lightning and reddened in the sky at twilight. He was handsome and could take on any form at will. Surrounded by heavenly ornaments, he looked like Mount Mandara slumbering with its trees, forests, and thickets. He had now ceased his dalliance for the night and left off his drinking. And there — adorned with costly jewellery — he lay, the beloved of the *rākṇasa* maidens and the bringer of delight to the *rākṣasas*. — 5.8.5-9[6]

Again later in the Sundara Kāṇḍa at *sarga* 47, Hanumān, as part of his intelligence gathering mission allows himself to be captured by the *rākṣasas*. As he is brought into the court he again decribes the lord of the demons:

> Then Hanumān gazed upon the immeasurably splendid lord of the *rākṣasas*, who sat before him like a rain-charged thundercloud resting on the peak of Mount Meru. With his priceless, glittering, golden crown set with masses of pearls, he was luminous and

5. Pollock 1991, pp. 150-51.
6. Goldman and Sutherland Goldman 1996, p. 135.

> resplendent. He wore exquisite, golden jewellery made up largely of priceless gems and fastened with diamond pins. They seemed to be creations of the imagination. He was clothed in costly silks and covered with red sandalpaste. His body was beautifully adorned with various lovely designs. With his ten large and beautiful heads each with red eyes, terrifying appearance, large, sharp, and shining fangs, and pendulous lips, that powerful hero was as splendid as Mount Mandara, its peaks filled with various savage beasts. Resembling a mass of black collyrium and with a sparkling necklace — its principal gemstone like the full moon — strung across his chest, he looked like a thundercloud crossed by a bright line of flying cranes. With their coating of fine sandalpaste, their armlets tightly fastened, and their bracelets flashing, his muscular arms resembled five-headed serpents. He was seated on a great and splendid crystal throne. It was exquisite, adorned with jewelled fastenings and covered with a magnificent cushion. He was closely attended by young women exquisitely ornamented, who stood all around him with yak-tail fly whisks in their hands. — 5.47-2-13[7]

While these passages highlight the physical prowess of the lord of the *rākṣasas*, they also clearly mark him as being ornamented with jewellery and compared to or surrounded by gold and jewels. But the description, especially the inclusion of the jewellery becomes more meaningful in the context of Vālmīki's description of Rāma. Compare for a moment, the opening passages of the Bāla Kāṇḍa, where the poet takes the opportunity to provide the audience with a detailed description of Rāma.

7. Goldman and Sutherland Goldman 1996, pp. 247-48.

His name is Rāma and he was born in the House of Ikṣvāku. All men know of him, for he is self-controlled, mighty, radiant, steadfast, and masterful. He is wise and grounded in proper conduct. Eloquent and majestic, he annihilates his enemies. His shoulders are broad and his arms mighty. His neck is like a conch-shell and his jaws are powerful. His chest is vast, and a subduer of his enemies, he wields a huge bow. His collarbone is set deep in muscle, his arms reach down to his knees, and his head is finely made. His brow is noble and his gait full of grace. His proportions are perfect and his limbs well-formed and symmetrical. Dark is his complexion and he is valorous. His chest is fully fleshed; he has large eyes. He is splendid and marked with all auspicious signs. He knows the ways of righteousness and is always true to his word. The welfare of his subjects is his constant concern. He is renowned, learned, pure, disciplined, and contemplative. He is the protector of all living things and the guardian of righteousness. Versed in the essence of the Vedas and their subsidiary sciences, he is equally expert in the science of arms. He is versed in the essence of every science, learned in traditional lore, and highly intelligent. All the people love him, for he is good, cheerful, and clever. He is the constant resort of good men, as is the ocean of rivers. For he is noble and equable in all circumstances and always a pleasure to behold. The delight of his mother Kauśalyā, he is gifted with every virtue. For he as deep as the ocean and as unyielding as the Himalayas. He is as mighty as Viṣṇu, but as pleasant to behold as the moon. In his wrath he resembles the fire at the end of time, yet he rivals the

> earth in forbearance. In charity he is the equal of Kubera, giver of wealth. . . . — 1.1.8-19[8]

What is noteworthy for our purposes is that despite the 'thick' description of the physical and psychological make-up of the hero, there is not one reference to his body being ornamented nor is he compared with any colours or images suggestive of ornamentation, such as 'golden' [R. Goldman 1984: 121-22]. Similar descriptive passages are repeated throughout the epic, especially in the Sundara Kāṇḍa, which focuses much attention, serving as a meditation, as it were, on the description of the absent hero.[9]

The contrast between the protagonist and the antagonist is marked and intentional. Rāma maintains the law, Rāvaṇa breaks it. Rāma is self-controlled, while Rāvaṇa abducts the wives of others. At the same time both passages draw on similar images, albeit for purposes of contrast, providing an almost uncanny parallelism between the two figures. For example, both, not unexpectedly, focus on the physical size and martial prowess of the figures: Rāma's 'chest is vast . . . he wields a huge bow. His collarbone is set deep in muscle, his arms reach down to his knees, and his head his finely made', while Rāvaṇa 'had twenty arms and ten necks. . . . A broad-chested, mighty king. . . . His arms were handsome, his teeth bright white, his mouth huge, and he was as tall as a mountain'. Viṣṇu appears in both passages, presaging the epic's final battle. Rāma 'is as mighty as Viṣṇu', while Rāvaṇa, 'in combat with gods his body had been wounded in hundreds of places by blows from Viṣṇu's discus. . . .' Similarly juxtaposed is the figure of Kubera: Rāvaṇa of course has conquered his

8. See too Ayodhyā Kāṇḍa, 1.10-28.
9. Goldman and Goldman 1996, pp.17-19 For an example of a detailed anatomical description of Rāma, see Sundara Kāṇḍa 33.

half-brother and taken his flying chariot Puṣpaka, while Rāma is said to be 'in charity the equal of Kubera, giver of wealth'. Both the antagonist and the protagonist are clearly great beings and worthy foes.[10] The virtual absence of any ornamentation in reference to Rāma — he seems, as it were, to be adorned with his virtues — when juxtaposed to the what appears as almost excessive and repeated identification of Rāvaṇa in terms of his ornamentation becomes more striking. Rāvaṇa has a golden throne, he looks 'like fire on a golden altar blazing with rich ornaments'. He 'sparkles' with earrings of burnished gold and glossy beryl. He wears 'exquisite, golden jewellery made up largely of priceless gems and fastened with diamond pins'. But, what does this contrast signify?

The wearing of jewellery is, of course, not limited to males or *rākṣasas*. Women, not unexpectedly, are commonly associated with jewellery. The poetic description of the wives of Rāvaṇa — women of all backgrounds, *yakṣas*, *gandharvas*, and the like — found in the Sundara Kāṇḍa is memorable for its erotic intensity as well as its careful attention to the women's of jewellery.[11]

> And there he saw reclining on the carpet a thousand beautiful women. They were wearing clothes and garlands of all different colours, and they wore every sort of dress and ornament. It was past midnight, and they had all succumbed to the power of drink and sleep. They had ceased their amorous play and now slept soundly in the dead of night. Lying there in slumber, the various sounds of their ornaments stilled,

10. Don't forget that Rāvaṇa is the abductor and ravager of women as well. See Sundara Kāṇḍa 5.7.5; 5.10.22 and Goldman and Goldman 1996, pp. 357, 583 and Uttara Kāṇḍa 17,24,26.
11. 5.7.30-63.

they collectively resembled a vast bed of lotuses whose *haṁsa*s and bees had fallen silent. — 5.7.30-33

The women lay there, their consciousness stolen by slumber. Their thick and heavy garlands were disordered, and their fine jewellery lay scattered about them from their bouts of drinking and physical exertions. Some of them had their *tilaka*s smudged, and some had their anklets all awry; while some of those beautiful women had their necklaces tossed to one side. The pearl necklaces of some had been broken; the garments of others had fallen away. Indeed, with their belt-strings snapped, they resembled young fillies relieved of their heavy loads. Some of them, wearing beautiful earrings, their garlands crushed and torn, resembled flowering creepers crushed by mighty elephants in the great forest. Splendid pearl necklaces — shining with the luster of moonbeams — rested like sleeping *haṁsa*s between the breasts of some of the women. The lapis lazuli necklaces that some wore looked like *kadamba* birds, while the gold chains of others resembled *cakravāka* birds. Their buttocks resembling sandbanks, the women looked like rivers crowded with *haṁsa*s and *kāraṇḍava*s and adorned with *cakravāka*s. With their masses of tiny bells for lotus buds and their large gold ornaments for full-blown lotuses, with their amorous gestures for crocodiles and their radiant beauty for banks, the sleeping women resembled rivers. The lovely marks left on some of them, impressed on their tender limbs and nipples by their ornaments, looked like the ornaments themselves.

— 5.7.41-49

> Some of those beautiful young women — all adorned with bracelets — lay cushioning their heads on their arms and on their lovely upper garments. — 5.7.56

The passage makes numerous references to the disarray of the women's ornamentation from their recent love-making. The description of these women, it can be argued, is in fact, structurally dependent upon their jewellery and ornaments. What is opaque in the passages describing Rāvaṇa and the other *rākṣasa*s mentioned by Pollock, is made clear in this passage: For here ornamentation is directly linked to sexual activity.

In this light Rāvaṇa's excessive association with jewellery and ornamentation discussed above is most apt. He is, after all, the character most marked by excess, particularly sexual excess.[12] The scene above describes his harem, his women, his sexual activities with the women, and his sexual excess. Contrasted with this is Rāma, a figure who is the paragon of sexual restraint. He has only one wife and unlike other males in the epic is willing to abandon her, even though she is innocent, for the sake of his kingdom.[13] To emphasise this Vālmīki leaves his hero largely unadorned.

That Vālmīki chooses to describe the women of Rāvaṇa's harem, fresh from their exertions of love-making, so densely in terms of their ornamentation becomes even more significant, if we examine the descriptions of other women in the epic. For not all women are associated with the wearing of ornaments. Take, for example, Kauśalyā, the senior wife of

12. In the Uttara Kāṇḍa, Rāvaṇa's sexual excess is again brought to the forefront. See for example Uttara Kāṇḍa 17, where Rāvaṇa ravishes Vedavatī, 24, where he abducts women and ravishes them, and 26 where he ravishes Rambhā.

13. Uttara Kāṇḍa 42-47 and Goldman and Sutherland Goldman 1996, pp. 70-74.

Daśaratha. Vālmīki has remarkably little to say about the physical appearance of this important figure. Kauṣalyā is a somewhat shadowy figure through much of the epic, one often mentioned but rarely seen or heard from. One of her major appearances, if not her main one, occurs in the Ayodhyā Kāṇḍa. When Rāma first comes to her, after hearing of his imminent coronation,

> Kauśalyā stood with her eyes closed . . . from the moment she received word the her son was to be consecrated as prince regent on Puṣya day, she had been controlling her breathing and meditation on the Primal Being, Janārdana.[14]

Then as Rāma comes to tell her that he is going to be banished, Vālmīki pauses to describe her as,

> Dressed in linen, intent upon her vow and with deep delight, she was then pouring an oblation into the fire in accordance with the vedic verses and pronouncing benedictions.[15]

The description is of a pious woman who has focused her energies and life on her son, rather than on her husband.[16] If one associates jewellery with sexual activity as suggested above, the absence of ornamentation or mention of jewellery can then be understood as intentional on the part of the poet. For, Kauśalyā is engaged in religious activities, and such activities are normally marked by sexual abstinence in the

---

14. 2.4.32-33.
15. 2.12.7.
16. This becomes an issue later as well, where Kauśalyā begs Rāma to take her to the forest, but he refuses because she is married and should stay and serve her husband. Ayodhyā Kāṇḍa 21, especialy verses 20-21.

tradition.[17] Moreover, as the elder wife she is no longer erotically favoured by her husband, Daśaratha, and has been replaced by a sexually active younger wife.[18] She has been located outside of the world of sexualities.

Now let us turn our attention to yet another group of women, women who like the women of Rāvaṇa's harem are described in great and graphic detail. These are the female guards of Sītā. They are *rākṣasīs*, and markedly dissimilar to the women described above:

> Straining to see Vaidehī, Hanumān, son of Mārut the wind god, saw — a short distance away — frightful-looking *rākṣasa* women. One had but one eye. One had but a single ear, while another's ears covered her entire upper body. One had no ears at all. Another had pointed ears, while yet another had her nose on her forehead. One had a huge head; another's neck was long and thin. One had hardly any hair, while another was completely bald. Yet another's hair covered her like a woollen blanket. One had pendulous ears and a bulbous forehead; another's breasts and belly hung down. One's lips protruded, while another's lips were on her chin. Yet another's mouth hung open, while still another's knees stuck out. One was very short; another very tall. One was hunchbacked, another was deformed, while yet another was a dwarf. One was snaggletoothed; another had a sunken face. One had yellow eyes, while another's features were distorted. The best of monkeys stared at those *rākṣasa* women, whose appearance caused his fur to bristle. They were deformed, yellowish, black, wrathful, fond of

17. Goldman 1998.
18. Sutherland 1991.

> quarrels, and armed with spears, mallets, and war-hammers of black iron. Some had the faces of boars, deer, tigers, buffalo, goats, or jackals. Some had feet like those of elephants, camels, and horses. Others' heads were sunk into their bodies. Some had only one hand; others one foot. Some had the ears of donkeys, horses, cows, elephants, or monkeys. Some had no noses; others had huge ones. Some had crooked noses or noses without nostrils. Some had noses like elephants' trunks, while others had nostrils in their foreheads. Some had the feet of elephants, some had enormous feet, some had feet like cows' hooves, and some had hairy feet. Some had enormous heads, necks, breasts, and bellies. Some had enormous mouths and eyes, while others had long tongues and nails. Some of those dreadful-looking *rākṣasa* women had the faces of goats, elephants, cows, sows, horses, camels, or donkeys. They held lances and war-hammers; and they were wrathful and fond of quarrels. Those *rākṣasa* women were snaggletoothed. Their hair was like smoke, and their faces were hideous. Addicted to meat and wine, they were constantly guzzling strong drink. Their bodies were smeared with flesh and blood, for such was their food. — 5.15.4-17[19]

The women here are grotesquely unattractive. They are working-class women, as it were, sharply differentiated form the attractive aristocratic women of Rāvaṇa's harem. This and the parallel passage at 5.20 provide a frame in which the unattractiveness of these women surrounds and contrast sharply with Sītā's delicate beauty,[20] which we will discuss

19. See Goldman and Goldman 1996, pp. 157-58. The women are described again in similar terms at 5.20.31-33.

20. Goldman, Forthcoming.

below. These grotesque and terrifying women are partly intended to serve as a foil for the heroine. Their terrifying mien and physical appearance are acutely brought to the forefront through their animal body parts, often anatomically misplaced. The passage leaves little to the imagination: these women are not intended to be physically attractive. Despite earlier associations of *rākṣasas* and the wearing of jewellery, here for these grotesquely asexual *rākṣasīs*, there is a marked lack of such ornamentation.[21]

That we can establish an association between the wearing of jewellery and sexual activity and desirability can be further attested by looking at the passage in which Kaikeyī, Bharata's mother, coerces her husband, Daśaratha, to give her two boons. The passage, found in the Ayodhyā Kāṇḍa, really starts with Mantharā, Kaikeyī's servant, arriving in a rage to tell Kaikeyī of Rāma's impending coronation. Kaikeyī throughout the passage is called golden and is described as wearing abundant and costly jewellery. Mantharā herself, like the *rākṣasīs* in Rāvaṇa's employment, is a working woman. She is deformed, a hunchback. At first, hearing her news, Kaikeyī is delighted[22] but Mantharā convinces Kaikeyī that her position in the harem is in danger (from Kauśalyā) if Rāma is made king. Finally succeeding in persuading her, Mantharā tells Kaikeyī what to do:

21. The only possessions mentioned of these women are their weapons, weapons of war, weapons that carry with them phallic symbolism (Sundara Kāṇḍa 22.10-11). Weapons are masculine implements for Vālmīki as testified to by the fact that Rāma and Rāvaṇa are described in terms of their weapons, and their prowess, their manliness as it were, is projected onto their weapons. For a description of male *rākṣasas*, who are members of Rāvaṇa's forces, see 5.3.29-33. Especially note verse 22, where they are said to be adorned with 'the finest ornaments [*varābharaṇabhāṣitān*]'.

22. Note that Kaikeyī gives Mantharā a piece of jewellery (2.7.28). See footnote below.

> Now go into your private chamber, daughter of Aśvapati, as if in a fit of rage. Put on a dirty garment, lie down on the bare ground, and don't speak to him, don't even look at him. — 2.9.16[23]

Incited by Mantharā, Kaikeyī then retreats to her private chamber, 'puffed up with the intoxicating power of her beauty':

> There the lovely lady removed her pearl necklace, worth many hundred thousands, and her other costly and beautiful jewellery. And then, under the spell of the hunchback Mantharā's words, the golden Kaikeyī got down upon the floor and said to her: 'Hunchback, go inform the king that I will surely die right here

---

23. The power of ornamentation to transform its possessor into an object of desire is perhaps most clearly demonstrated in Kaikeyī's promised rewards to Mantharā. Here, Mantharā, deformed and marked as evil because of that deformity, virtually takes on a new persona once she is marked with jewellery and associated with the colour gold.

    Kaikeyī, pleased with Mantharā, says:

    'There are hunchbacks who are misshapen, crooked and hideously ugly — but not you, you are lovely, you are bent no more than a lotus in the breeze. Your chest is arched, raised as high as your shoulders, and down below your waist, with its lovely navel, seems as if it had grown thin in envy of it. Your girdle-belt beautifies your hips and sets them tingling. Your legs are set strong under you, while your feet are long. With your wide buttocks, Mantharā, and your garment of white linen, you are as resplendent as a wild goose when you go before me. And this huge hump of yours, wide as the hub of a chariot wheel — your clever ideas must be stored in it, your political wisdom and magic powers. And there, hunchback, is where I will drape you with a garland made of gold, once Bharata is consecrated and Rāghava has gone to the forest. When I have accomplished my purpose, my lovely, when I am satisfied, I will anoint your hump with precious liquid gold. And for your face I will have them fashion an elaborate and beautiful forehead mark of gold and exquisite jewellery for you, hunchback. Dressed in a pair of lovely garments you shall go about like a goddess; with that face of yours that challenges the moon, peerless in visage; and you shall strut holding your head high before the people who hate me (2.930-38).

> unless Bharata receives as his portion the land and Rāghava, as his, the forest.' And uttering these ruthless words, the lady put all her jewelry aside and lay down upon the ground bare of any spread, like a fallen *kinnara* woman. — 2.9.43-46

As soon as Daśaratha has given the orders for Rāma's coronation, he retreats to Kaikeyī's private chambers, the expected site of sexual activity. Daśaratha enters only find his beloved on the floor; he is filled with sorrow and begins to caress her. He promises to do anything for her, even if it costs him his life.[24] The removal of jewellery, the lying down on the floor, and the wearing of a 'dirty' garment, mark Kaikeyī as unattractive, that is sexually unappealing or unavailable; and Daśaratha immediately understands the message.

> I do not understand, my lady, why you should be angry. Has someone offended you, or shown you disrespect, that you should lie here in the dust, my precious, and cause me such sorrow? What reason have you to lie upon the floor as if possessed by a spirit, driving me to distraction, when you are so precious to me? — 2.10.6-7

> I and my people, we all bow to your will. I could not bring myself to thwart any wish of yours, not if it cost me my life. Tell me what your heart desires, for all the earth belongs to me, as far as the wheel of my power reaches. — 2.10.11-12

The epic makes it clear that Daśaratha is infatuated with his young wife, willing to do anything to keep her happy. Kaikeyī's removal of her jewellery sends an unmistakable message to her husband that she is not sexually available and

24. 2.10.11-12.

will not be until her demands are satisfied. Only then will she put on her ornaments and be available to him.

Perhaps the issue that becomes most significant and puzzling in this discussion of the symbolic association of sexual activity and jewellery is that of Sītā's possession of jewellery during her exile and, in particular, of her special crest-jewel ornament (*cūḍāmaṇi*) that she has secreted away during her abduction and imprisonment.

This issue of Sītā's jewels is very complex. When Rāma, Lakṣmaṇa, and Sītā leave Ayodhyā, Kaikeyī makes it clear that they are to abandon all wealth before they go into exile. Before departing, Rāma and Sītā give away their belongings, including their jewellery, to various dependents and brāhmaṇas.[25] As they take their leave of their father, Kaikeyī insists that the threesome give up their finery and dress in barkcloth, the garb of ascetics. In a touching scene, an embarrassed Sītā asks her husband, 'How do the sages who live in the forest put on barkcloth?'[26] And,

> At once Rāma, champion of righteousness, came up to her and with his own hands fastened it over Sītā's silks. — 2.33.12

Note the poignancy of the passage as Rāma places the barkcloth over Sītā's silken garments, a symbolic covering up, as it were of sexual activity. Sītā like Rāma is suppose to abandon her finery for a life of restraint and deprivation in the forest. But Daśaratha relents at the last minute, and orders Sumantra to 'fetch precious garments and choice ornaments for Vaidehī, calculating against the number of years'.[27] Then,

---

25. 2.28.18-20-2.29.
26. 2.33.10.
27. 2.34.15.

> Noble Vaidehī, on the point of leaving for the forest, adorned her noble limbs with sparkling jewellery.
>
> — 2.34.17

Later, at the end of the Ayodhyā Kāṇḍa, Anasūyā, wife of Atri presents Sītā with gifts of 'raiment, cream, jewellery, and garlands'.[28] The issue arises as to why Rāma and Lakṣmaṇa are sent off in barkcloth garments, garments that represent restraint, poverty, cẹlibacy, but Sītā is allowed to wear silk, and jewellery, signs that mark beauty and sexuality. The answer in part can be attributed to a gender bias; men are stronger and can withstand the hardships of life, whereas women are weak (*abalā*). More importantly, however, is the fact that the plot of Vālmīki's epic cannot move forward without Sītā going to the forest,[29] and moreover she must be represented as a sexually viable/desirable figure. She needs to be attractive enough to have Rāvaṇa desire to abduct her. The jewels given to her by Daśaratha and Anasūyā symbolically provide Sītā with such erotic viability.

In the Araṇya Kāṇḍa, the presence and absence of jewellery become more clearly symbolic. We have already heard Vālmīki's dense description of Rāvaṇa discussed above. But, when Rāvaṇa comes to abduct Sītā, he is disguised as a wandering mendicant, a holy man, 'he had come in the garb of a twice-born brāhmaṇa with a begging bowl and saffron robe'; when she saw these accoutrements, it was impossible to refuse him, and so she extended him an invitation befitting

28. 2.110.20.

29. *Adhyātma Rāmāyaṇa* 2.4.77-78 acknowledges this itself, when Sītā begging Rāma to let her accompany him to the story, finally falls back upon the story itself, and says, 'I will tell you something else, which having heard, you will take me to the forest. Repeatedly *Rāmāyaṇa*s have been heard by many twice-borns; You tell me in which one does Rāma go to the forest without Sītā? Therefore, I will go with you as your companion in every way.' See too Ramanujan 1991, p. 33.

a brāhmaṇa.[30] He presents himself as someone who has given up the pleasures of life, someone whom Sītā, although vulnerable, should not have to fear. He has taken off his fine garb and his ornamentation, and is marked as an asexual figure.

Sītā, however, is described in very feminine, in fact in very sexual, terms. Even her garments of yellow silk reflect the colour of her jewels. They are of fine luxurious material, not linen like that of Kauśalyā, they are yellow, later called 'golden', and, like golden jewellery, are compared to lightning.[31]

But the words Vālmīki has Rāvaṇa use to describe Sītā are such as to leave no doubt in the audiences' mind of his intentions despite his garb:

> Who are you, golden woman dressed in garments of yellow silk, wearing a lovely lotus garland, and like a lotus pond yourself? Are you the goddess Modesty or Fame? Are you Śrī or lovely Lakṣmī or perhaps an *apsaras*, lovely lady? Could you be Prosperity, shapely woman, or easygoing Pleasure? Your teeth are bright white, tapered, and even; your eyes are large and clear, rosy at the corner, black in the centre. Your hips are full and broad, your thighs smooth as an elephant's trunk. And these, your delightful breasts, how round they are, so firm and gently heaving; how full and lovely, smooth as two palm fruits, with their nipples standing stiff and the rarest gems to adorn them. Graceful lady with your lovely smile, lovely teeth and lovely eyes, you have swept my heart away like a river in flood that sweeps away its banks. Your waist I could compass with my fingers; how fine is your hair, how

30. 3.44.33.
31. 3.50.13

> firm your breasts. No goddess, no *gandharva* woman, no *yakṣa* or *kinnara* woman, nor mortal woman so beautiful have I ever seen before on the face of this earth. Your beauty, unrivalled in all the worlds, your delicacy and youth, and the fact of your living here in the woods stir the deepest feelings in me. I urge you to go home, this is no place for you to be living. For this is the lair of the dreaded *rākṣasa*s, who can change their form at will. In the most delightful palaces, in luxuriant, fragrant city gardens is where you should be strolling. To my mind you deserve the finest garlands and beverages and raiment, and the finest husband, lovely black-eyed lady. Could you be one of the Rudras or Maruts, sweet-smiling shapely woman, or one of the Vasus, perhaps. You look like a goddess to me. — 3.44.15-26

Like Kaikeyī, she is 'golden',[32] her breasts are 'delightful, round, so firm and gently heaving; full and lovely, smooth as two palm fruits', and adorned with 'the rarest gems'. The passage is as physically and sexually explicit as Vālmiki's epic gets, comparing in tone to that of Sundara Kāṇḍa discussed above.[33]

Rāvaṇa then reveals his own true form:

> With eyes flaming bright red, with earrings of burnished gold, with bow and arrows, he became once more the majestic ten-faced stalker of the night.
>
> — 3.47.6

32. Sītā and Kaikeyī are both described as golden. Later, Sītā is again called 'golden' by Rāvaṇa at 3.45.23 'Now that I have set eyes on you, flawless, golden lady dressed in silk, I shall no longer take any pleasure in my own wives.' Mandodarī, the chief queen of Rāvaṇa, is also described as 'golden-skinned' (5.8.48). It is clearly a trait of sexually-viable, attractive women (and men).

33. See too Rāvaṇa's seduction of Sītā in the Sundara Kāṇḍa 5.18.

> With eyes flaming bright red in his rage, lowering like a bank of storm clouds, clad in a red garment Rāvaṇa stood before Maithilī, staring at her, perfect jewel of a woman, with her jet-black hair, her sunlike radiance, and the fine clothes and ornaments that she wore.
>
> — 3.47.9-10

Note that Rāvaṇa's true form, the form in which he will abduct Sītā, requires that he be ornamented with 'earrings of burnished gold'. Sītā's finery is not neglected either at this most crucial moment of the epic; not only is she a 'perfect jewel' of a woman, but she is wearing fine clothes and ornaments. Moreover, she is once again associated with the colour gold, for her radiance is 'sunlike'.

As Rāvaṇa carries her up into the sky in his chariot, Sītā is again described:

> All adorned in ornaments of burnished gold and dressed in garments of yellow silk, the princess looked like a streak of lightning flashing from a storm cloud.
>
> — 3.50.13

A few verses later,

> Maithilī was golden skinned, the *rākṣasa* deep blue-black, and folded within his arms she looked like the star that glitters within a sapphire. Fair as a lotus, golden hued, with ornaments of burnished gold, the daughter of Janaka in Rāvaṇa's embrace looked like a streak of lightning caught within a storm cloud. The sound of Vaidehī's ornaments made the overlord of the *rākṣasas* still more like a rain cloud, pure blue-black and now sounding as well. — 3.50.21-23

Here Sītā is compared to a 'star that glitters within a sapphire', again she is golden, and now, like Rāvaṇa, has 'ornaments of burnished gold'. But as she is dragged into the sky, her ornaments begin to fall off:

> Vaidehī's jewel-studded anklet was shaken from her foot, and gently tinkling it fell like an arc of lightning. . . . — 3.50.27
>
> Her flame-coloured ornaments were scattered noisily upon the ground, falling like stars from the firmament when their store of merit has been exhausted. Shining like the moon, the overlord of stars, Vaidehī's pearl necklace slipped from between her breasts and fell like the white Ganges descending from heaven.
> — 3.50.30-31

What is the significance of Sītā's ornaments falling off at this particular juncture in the epic story? Or do they actually fall off? Here the inference is that the jewels actually slip off, but at the beginning of *sarga* 52, she removes them intentionally:

> The large-eyed, shapely Maithilī dropped her golden silk shawl among them, and her lovely ornaments, in hopes they might tell Rāma. She unfastened her garment and let it fall with her jewellery among them, but the ten-necked Rāvaṇa was too wild with excitement to notice she had done so. — 3.52.2-3

Sītā is sending a message to Rāma. Moreover, it is an action that Rāvaṇa, it seems, would have prevented had he seen it, but he is too excited to notice. The narrative use of the jewellery is clear. The fallen ornaments can provide a clue for Rāma. The symbolism of the falling off of or the removal of the jewellery of Sītā becomes more meaningful in light of the present discussion. For, again like Kaikeyī and Kauśalyā, once deprived of ornaments, Sītā is no longer sexually available or viable. Her symbolic sexuality is left behind, as it were, in Rāma's keeping.[34]

Rāma searches the forest for Sītā, and finally at the beginning of the Kiṣkindhā Kāṇḍa, when he meets Sugrīva and Hanumān, he is told that the monkeys have found her golden ornaments. The monkeys have carefully protected the jewellery, keeping them secreted deep in a mountain cave:

> The monkey took the shawl and bright ornaments and showed them to Rāma, saying, 'look at this'. Then, as Rāma took that garment and the bright ornaments, tears covered his face as mist covers the moon. His face was stained with tears he shed for love of Sītā. Crying, 'Ah, beloved', he lost his composure and fell to the ground. Repeatedly he pressed those fine ornaments to his heart and sighed deeply like an angry snake in its burrow. Through an unbroken stream of tears, Rāma saw Saumitri by his side and began to lament piteously: Look, Lakṣmaṇa, here are the shawl and ornaments that Vaidehī let fall from her body to the ground as she was being carried away.
>
> — 4.6.13-18

Rāma's reaction to the jewellery and garment is one of physical intensity. He presses it to his body, as if caressing it. Finally, the sight of it causes him to 'lose his composure'. He laments piteously.

The narrative significance of the discarded jewellery is once again noted, this time by Rāma. Vālmīki also makes it

34. I would argue that the monkeys are important here as well, as they are associated with 'sexuality' and aggressive sexual behaviour (R. Goldman 1989). It is no accident that the monkeys keep the jewels hidden in a cave.

clear that Rāma understands its symbolic meaning as well. For, he says to Lakṣmaṇa,

> As she was being carried off, Sītā must surely have dropped these ornaments onto grassy ground, and that is why they look like this. — 4.6.19

What exactly does the phrase, 'that is why they look like this', (*tathārūpam*) mean here? And what is the significance of Rāma saying it? The commentators are in agreement that the ornaments look as they always had, that is to say they are undamaged. According to Govindarāja, they are undamaged because they fell in a soft place. Moreover, according to him, Rāma is surprised, it seems, that the ornaments are intact. The fact that the jewels are not broken or damaged, as they are in the Sundara Kāṇḍa scene after the violent love-making scene of the women in the harem, would argue for Sītā's sexuality being left intact, as it were, that is to say, not violated or damaged.

At this juncture in the epic, the southern or vulgate version of the epic inserts a well-known verse, which for the purposes of our discussion is very significant. Lakṣmaṇa, being asked to identify the jewellery, responds:

> I do not recognise these armlets, I do not recognise these earrings. But I do recognise these anklets because of my constant bowing at her feet.[35]

This oft-quoted verse makes clear that Lakṣmaṇa's devotion to and total subservience to his older brother, Rāma, is so great that he would not even look at his brother's wife. Such

---

35. 4.147*, lines 3, 4:
nāhaṁ jānāmi keyūre nāhaṁ jānāmi kuṇḍale ।
nūpure tv abhijānāmi nityaṁ pādābhivandanāt ॥

a look would have sexual connotations.[36] That he cannot recognise her armlets and her earrings plays on this understanding and further strengthens the argument for the connection between sexuality and the wearing of jewellery.

Jewellery once more becomes a focal index of sexuality in the Sundara Kāṇḍa, the fifth book of the epic. Here Hanumān finds the abducted heroine in Rāvaṇa's pleasure garden. It is attached to the *antaḥpuram*, or harem, and is marked as a site of sexual activity.[37] Here the beautiful and touching description of Sītā as she languishes in the *aśoka* garden stands in stark contrast to not only her surroundings but to earlier descriptions of her. The passage is remarkable for is poetry, some of the finest in the epic, for its pathos, and for its seemingly utter inconsistency and confusion over Sītā's jewellery.

As Hanumān searches the garden and its environs,

> Then he saw a woman clad in a soiled garment and surrounded by *rākṣasa* women. She was gaunt with fasting. She was dejected and she sighed repeatedly. She looked like the shining sliver of the waxing moon. Her radiance was lovely; but with her beauty now only faintly discernible, she resembled a flame of fire occluded by thick smoke. She was clad in a single, fine yellow garment, now much worn. Covered with dirt and lacking ornaments, she resembled a pond without lotuses. Ashamed, tormented by grief, disconsolate, and suffering, she looked like the constellation Rohiṇī occluded by the planet Mars. She was dejected, her face covered with tears. She was emaciated through fasting. She was depressed, given over to sorrow.

36. Goldman 1997.

37. Goldman, Forthcoming.

> Brooding constantly, she was consumed with her grief. No longer seeing the people dear to her but only the hosts of *rākṣasa* women, she was like a doe cut off from her herd and surrounded by a pack of hounds. She had a single braid-like a black serpent-falling down her back. Deserving only happiness and unaccustomed to calamity, she was consumed with sorrow. Closely examining that wide-eyed woman so dirty and emaciated — he reasoned from these indicative signs, 'She must be Sītā!' — 5.13.18-25

The description is one that evokes great pathos in the audience, she is covered with dirt, wearing a single soiled garment and above all lacking ornaments. She is like an ascetic woman meditating on her lord. But our heroine must have some redeeming features, for not only did the antagonist abduct her, but her husband is willing to literally go to the ends of the earth to find her. Hanumān continues:

> 'This woman looks exactly like the one I saw earlier being carried off by that *rākṣasa,* who can take on any form at will.' Sītā's face was like the full moon; her eyebrows were beautiful; her breasts were lovely and full. With her radiance that lady banished the darkness from all directions. Her hair was jet black; her lips like bimba fruit. Her waist was lovely, and her posture was perfect. Her eyes were like lotus petals, and she looked like Rati, wife of Manmatha, god of love.
>
> — 5.13.26-28

But again we are reminded that though beautiful, she is still virtuous and faithful:

> That lovely woman — as cherished by all living things as the radiance of the full moon — was seated on the

ground like an ascetic woman practising austerity. Sighing constantly, that timorous woman resembled a daughter-in-law of a serpent lord. By virtue of the vast net of sorrow spread over her, her radiance was dimmed like that of a flame of fire obscured by a shroud of smoke. She was like a blurred memory or a fortune lost. She was like faith lost or hope dashed, like success undermined by catastrophe or intellect dulled. She was like a reputation lost through false rumors. She was distraught at being prevented from rejoining Rāma and anguished by her abduction by the *rākṣasa*. That delicate, fawn-eyed woman was looking about here and there. Her sorrowful face with its black-tipped eyelashes was covered with a flood of tears. She sighed again and again. Dejected, covered with dirt and grime, and devoid of ornaments — though she was worthy of them — she resembled the light of the moon, the king of stars, obscured by a black storm cloud. As he examined Sītā closely, Hanumān's mind was once more afflicted with uncertainty; for she seemed barely discernible, like some Vedic text once learned by heart but now nearly lost through lack of recitation. It was only with great difficulty that Hanumān was able to recognise Sītā without her ornaments, just as one might make out the sense of a word whose meaning had been changed through want of proper usage. Still, after closely examining the wide-eyed, blameless princess, he concluded that this was indeed Sītā, confirming his judgement through the tell-tale signs.

— 5.13.29-38

Yet again, we are reminded of Sītā's perfect beauty:

> Then he noticed on Vaidehī's body — beautifying her limbs — the mass of jewellery that Rāma had described. 'Though blackened with long use, her beautifully formed earrings, her finely crafted 'dog's teeth', and the handsome jewellery on her hands, variegated with gemstones and coral, are all in their proper places. I think they must be the very ones that Rāma described. I do not see the ones that fell back there, but those that have not fallen off are undoubtedly the very ones described by Rāma. Then, caught in a tree, where she had let it fall, the monkeys spied her splendid, yellow upper garment. It looked like a sheet of gold. On the ground they also found the large, jingling pieces of jewellery that she had thrown down. Although this garment of hers is exceedingly worn from long use, still, surely, it is the same splendid colour as the other. This must be Rāma's beloved golden-hued queen, who, though she is lost to him, has not departed from his heart.' — 5.13.39-46

The passage appears problematic. At verses 20, 35, and 37 she is described as having no ornaments, yet here two verses after this last mention of a lack of ornamentation, we are given a detailed inventory of Sītā's jewellery. Does Vālmīki nod? Or is the use of the jewellery here more symbolic? The verses are all well attested and solidly belong to the critical edition. It is equally doubtful that Vālmīki forgot so quickly that Sītā was lacking ornaments or was an unsophisticated poet.[38] If one looks more closely at the structure of the passage, an internal logic appears, one that allows the seemingly contradictory

38. The commentators themselves are at pains to explain away the seeming contradiction.

presence and absence of the jewellery to be understood.[39] The passage fluctuates between describing Sītā on the one hand as a woman who is sexually restrained and on the other as and sexually available. Thus in verses 18-25, we are given a description of Sītā as she appears in the *aśoka vana*, like an ascetic woman, thus 'lacking ornaments', but in verse 26-28, Hanumān reminds us of the woman he saw being abducted. Verses 29-38 again locate us in the *aśoka vana*, and again an ascetic, asexual Sītā is described. Verses 39-42 highlight the perfect beauty of the heroine, but note that her description in these verses, as in verses 26-28, is carefully framed to refer back to an earlier time, the time when Rāma last saw her, before her abduction. Finally, verses 39-46 present her again in the *aśoka vana*, but now the jewels and gold, silken garments are removed from her body.

The jewellery is absent just in those places in which Sītā's sexuality must be understood as repressed, while, when

---

39. The discussion occurs on the commentary to 5.13.39 (See Goldman and Goldman 1996, p. 394; notes on 13.39). Kaṭaka, on the other hand, vigorously repudiates this reading and the inferences that underlie it. He defends his reading as *pāṅktaḥ*, 'authentic', and denounces the reading of Maheśvaratīrtha and Govindarāja as ridiculous and contradictory to the stated facts. He argues that if Sītā had really divested herself of the jewellery described by Rāma and placed it on a high branch, then Hanumān, not seeing them, would have inferred that this was clearly not Sītā. Moreover, he argues, the following verses make it very clear that she is wearing her jewellery. He refutes the contention of Govindarāja and Maheśvaratīrtha that Sītā would have removed her jewellery in the conventional gesture of grieving for a lover from whom one is separated, on the grounds that her jewellery, like the earrings and armour of Karṇa, were born with her and were thus apparently not to be removed. He adds further that it would have been impossible for her [in her present circumstances] to have placed the ornaments anywhere with confidence. Finally, he notes that she would have kept her jewellery on as a means of recognition, if, by chance, an emissary [of Rāma] should come. It may be noted, however, that Nāgojībhaṭṭa seems not to object to the several passages in which Sītā is unambiguously described as being devoid of ornamentation.

Hanumān describes her as potentially sexual, i.e., as the rightful wife of Rāma, she is depicted as wearing jewellery or being associated with it. At least some of the commentators, who are generally unconcerned with this issue, indirectly support this in their comments to verse 39. The phrase, 'beautifying her limbs', is troublesome to them, as they are apparently worried about the presence of jewellery on Sītā. The word 'limbs' (*gātra*), in the critical edition in verse 39 is marked as uncertain. The commentators aligned with Govindarāja, i.e., Maheśvaratīrtha, Rāmānuja, and Uḍāli read instead *śākhā*, 'branch', thus reading 'beautify a branch'. In commenting on this verse, Maheśvaratīrtha notes,

> By this expression ('beautifying a branch') we are to understand that because of the impropriety of wearing jewellery while separated from Rāma, Sītā had removed her ornaments and placed them on a branch.

Govindarāja has a similar explanation. Even so, the true potency of the jewellery cannot be allowed and it is 'blackened', or tarnished so that it is present but occluded.

Before concluding, I would like to examine one more scene, a scene central to the epic narrative, in light of the above discussion. At *sarga* 36 of the Sundara Kāṇḍa, during the conversation between Sītā and Hanumān, Sītā gives Hanumān a special token of recognition to take to Rāma, it is her hair ornament, her *cūḍāmaṇi*. Giving Hanumān her message to Rāma, she says:

> 'You must rescue me, my hero, whom wicked Rāvaṇa has imprisoned through deceit, just as Kauśikī was rescued from the underworld Pātāla.' Then, taking out an exquisite, heavenly hair ornament she had kept wrapped in her garment, Sītā gave it to Hanumān with

> the words, 'You must give this to Rāghava'. The heroic monkey took that unsurpassed and magnificent gem and placed it on his finger, for he could not put it on his arm. — 5.36.51-52

That this piece of jewellery is a hair ornament is particularly significant in this context.[40] Hair and how it is worn are symbolic of sexuality.[41] Thus women whose husbands are alive and well wear their hair ornamented and well coifed. When one's husband is away or departed one wears one's hair in a style called the *ekaveṇī*, one single plait down the back. Untied and unkempt hair, like that of *rākṣasīs*, indicates unrestrained sexuality. The grabbing of hair, especially of women's hair is equated with sexual assault (note that Rāvaṇa grabs Sītā's hair in 3.47.16). Thus, the fact that Sītā's ornament has been secreted away even more intensely associates it with sexual activity.

This hair ornament, we are to learn in the next *sarga*, has a history and is very special to both Sītā and Rāma, for she tells Hanumān that the jewel 'will remind Rāma of three people: my mother, King Daśaratha, and myself' (5.37.2). Of all her jewellery, this piece is most prized by Sītā: It is the one, unlike the others, that has not been discarded, or lost, or even tarnished. Instead it has been kept hidden away wrapped inside of Sītā's garments where no one could see it. It is the jewel that only the closest members of her family know about, her mother, her father-in-law and her husband.[42]

---

40. For a discussion of the significance of hair in the Asian context, see Miller and Hitebeitel 1998.

41. Hara 1986.

42. There is, surprisingly, a considerable amount of confusion and disagreement as to the identity of the three people of whom Rāma is to be reminded by seeing the ornament. The verse appears to lend itself most easily to the reading we have given it, and this reading is also →

Now in the context of the epic narrative, Sītā has already provided Hanumān with an *abhijñāna*, or a token of recognition,

→ proposed by Śiromaṇi who states that in a story told in the Purāṇas, Sītā's mother presents Sītā with the jewel in Daśaratha's presence at the time of her marriage to Rāma. Among the translations consulted, we find this interpretation in Shastri (1957, p. 430), Raghunathan (1981, p. 437), and Roussel (1903, p. 582). The wording of *pāda*s cd, however, is not entirely unambiguous. Since the poet has chosen to use the *karmaṇi śeṣe ṣaṣṭhī*, 'the objective genitive', to denote the object of Rāma's recollection, it is difficult to distinguish among the four terms in this case or between the objective genitive and possible partitive genitive. Thus, the words *jananyā mama* can mean either 'my mother' or 'mother and me'. If one selects the latter reading, it is then not clear whether the reference is to Sītā's mother or Rāma's. In addition, the words *rājño daśarathasya* can mean either 'King Daśaratha' or 'the king [i.e., Janaka] and Daśaratha'. As a result of this ambiguity, the commentators have compiled a number of different lists, sometimes criticising the formulations proposed by others. Nāgojībhaṭṭa states: 'At the time of the wedding of Sītā and Rāma, her father [Janaka] took the jewel from the hand of her mother [Janaka's wife], who then placed it in the hand of Daśaratha to be Sītā's hair ornament'. 'Thus', he concludes, 'these are the three people Rāma will remember [i.e., Sītā's mother, Janaka, and Daśaratha]'. Maheśvaratīrtha slightly modifies Nāgojībhaṭṭa's tale of the gem's history. He claims that 'Sītā's mother took it from Janaka's hand in Daśaratha's presence and gave it directly to Sītā'. Therefore, he concludes, 'the people of whom it will be a reminder are Sītā's mother, Daśaratha, Janaka, and Sītā herself.' This is a reasonable proposition, except for the disquieting fact that the list of three now contains four names. Evidently what Maheśvaratīrtha means to suggest is that the jewel will remind Rāma of those three people as well as of Sītā herself. Govindarāja mentions two possible lists, rejecting one as incorrect. His notion of the gem's transmission is as follows: 'At the time of the marriage, Sītā's parents gave her the ring; and she accepted it. Therefore, the three people would be Janaka, Janaka's wife, and Sītā.' Govindarāja, however, goes on to say, 'At the wedding ceremony itself, the gem was first formally presented by her mother-in-law and father-in-law [i.e., Kauśalyā and Daśaratha] to Sītā to place in her hair.' Daśaratha, Kauśalyā, and Sītā would then constitute the threesome. This is, in fact, the list found in Dutt (1892, p. 1006), Tapasyānanda (1983, p. 170), and Simon (1934, p. 148). Govindarāja ascribes this latter list to an unnamed commentator and rejects it as inconsistent with two other pieces of data. These are (1) that according to the version of the story mentioned by Rāma later (5.64.4 = 5.66.4 GPP), the gem was given to Sītā by his in-laws (i.e., Janaka and Janaka's wife); and (2) according to Govindarāja, Rāma's mother was not present at the wedding. See 5.64.4-5. Cf. 5.26.8.

to give Rāma: in the form of the intimate narrative of the crow.[43] Why then is there need for a second *abhijñāna*, or is this second token merely redundant? Let us momentarily re-examine the larger context of the Hanumān-Sītā episode — Hanumān initially provides Sītā with a verbal testimony that he is a messenger of Rāma, by reciting the history of and description of Rāma, secondly he gives Sītā Rāma's signet ring, an implement with which one marks possessions. Sītā is, as it were, marked as belonging to Rāma. In return, Sītā first provides as a token of recognition for Rāma, a parallel oral testimony, the story of the crow. The story is intimate; one which only Rāma and Sītā (and the crow) know about. Secondly, Sītā provides her most precious jewel, her *cūḍāmaṇi*, clearly a parallel token to Rāma's signet ring, but one that has a substantially different meaning. For this jewel represents the closest and most intimate location, secreted away on her body, wrapped in her garments, one known only to a few people. This is no ordinary jewel, but one that sends a clear message to Rāma that Sītā has protected and hidden her sexuality. She has saved it for her lord and husband. For Vālmīki then, the *cūḍāmaṇi* is the quintessential marker of Sītā's sexual viability — protected by her mother, passed on to her father-in-law and then to husband, kept hidden away during her abduction and imprisonment until it could be returned to her husband. As Sītā gives the jewel to Hanumān, the transfer signals for the audience the symbolic return of Sītā or rather of her sexuality to Rāma, and so marks the turning point of the epic. Vālmīki can thus symbolically allow his heroine to be 'sexual' provided that her sexuality is hidden and kept intact to be returned to her husband.

---

43. Sundara Kāṇḍa 5.36.12-32, 65.2-17. See Goldman and Sutherland Goldman 1996, pp. 10-11, 216-18, 292-293, 454-58, 540-41.

If we return momentarily to Pollock's original question, we can now acknowledge that there is a clear significance to the seemingly excessive association of *rākṣasas* and jewellery. It is not accidental that women and *rākṣasas* are most frequently associated with such ornamentation. Women are traditionally considered hyper-sexualised beings, so are *rākṣasas* — traditionally defined as: *nārī pratyakṣarākṣasī* (a woman is nothing but a *rākṣasī*); and the jewellery they wear becomes symbolic of that sexuality. This association is not accidental on the part of Vālmīki but is integral to the internal logic of his larger narrative. It is one that, taken in a larger context, shows a pattern that is consistent and meaningful throughout the epic. It is only for us as *rasikas* of the poem and students of the epic to pause long enough to appreciate that narrative logic.

Bibliography

Ayyangar, C. R. Sreenivasa, tr., *The Rāmāyaṇa of Vālmīki*, vol. 2, *Sundarakanda and Yuddhakanda*, Madras: The Little Flower Co., 1991.

Bandhu, Vishva, *Rāmāyana*, vols. 7, 12, 14, 17-20, Lahore: D.A.V. College Sanskrit Series, 1947.

Bhatt, G.H. and U.P. Shah, *The Vālmīki Rāmāyaṇa: Critical Edition*, Baroda: Oriental Institute, 1975.

Dutt, M.N., tr., *The Rāmāyana*, vol. 5, *Sundara Kāndam*, Calcutta: Girish Chandra Chackravarti, 1892.

Gita Press Edition tr., 1969, See *Śrīmad Vālmīki Rāmāyaṇa*, 1969.

Goldman, Robert P. (ed. & tr.), *The Rāmāyaṇa of Vālmīki: An Epic of Ancient India*, vol. 1, *Bālakāṇḍa*, Princeton: Princeton University Press, 1984.

———, 'Tracking the Elusive Kṛṣṇa', *Journal of the American Oriental Society*, 109:4, 1989, pp. 545-52.

Goldman, Robert and Sally J. Sutherland Goldman, *The Rāmāyaṇa of Vālmīki: An Epic of Ancient India*, vol. 5, *Sundarakāṇḍa*, Princeton: Princeton University Press, 1996.

———, 'Vālmīki's Hanumān: Characterisation and Occluded Divinity in the Rāmāyaṇa', *Journal of Vaiṣṇava Studies*, 2:4, 1994, pp. 31-54.

Goldman, Sally J. Sutherland, 'The Power of the Gaze: Scopophilic Behaviour in Sanskrit Narrative', Paper presented at the conference 'Re-Presenting

Women: Workshop on Women in the Literary, Performing, and Visual Arts of India' at the University of California at Berkeley, 25-27 April 1997.

———, 'Soul Food: Consumption, Conception, and Gender in Early Sanskrit Literary Texts'. Paper presented at the University of California at Berkeley, May, 1998.

———, 'Sītā Speaks: The Voice of the Heroine in Sundarakāṇḍa of the Vālmīki Rāmāyaṇa', in Paula Richman (ed.), *Questioning Rāmāyaṇas: Gender, Politics and Multiple Perspectives within a South Asian Narrative Tradition*, 2000.

———, (forthcoming) 'Re-siting Sītā: Gender and Narrative in Vālmīki's Sundarakāṇḍa', in Mary McGee (ed.), *Sita in the City*.

Gorresio, Gaspare (ed.), *Ramayana, poema indiano di Valmici*, Paris: Stamperia Reale, 1867.

———, tr., *Ramayana, poema sanscrito di Valmici*, vols. 8, 9, Paris: Stamperia Reale, 1856.

Griffith, Ralph T. H., tr., *The Rāmāyaṇa of Vālmīki: Translated into English Verse*, vol. 4, London: Trübner and Co., 1873.

Hara, Minoru, 'The Holding of the Hair (Kesa-grahana)', in Soeren Egerod (ed.), *Acta Orientalia*, XLVII, Copenhagen: Munksgaard, 1986, pp. 67-92.

Hiltebeitel, Alf, 'Draupadī's Garments', *IIJ* 22, 1980, pp. 97-112.

———, 'Draupadī's Hair', *Puruṣārtha* 5, 1981, pp. 179-214.

———, 'Sītā Vibhūṣitā: The Jewels for her Journey', *Indologica Taurinensia*, vol. 8, 9. 1981, pp. 193-200.

Iyengar, K. R. Srinivasa, tr., *The Epic Beautiful: An English Verse Rendering of the Sundara Kanda of the Ramayana of Valmiki*, Delhi: Sahitya Akademi, 1983.

Krishnacharya, T. R. and T. R. Vyasacharya (eds.), *Śrīmad Vālmīki-Rāmāyanaṁ*, The Kumbakonam Edition, Bombay: Nirṇayasāgar Press, 1913.

Lefeber, Rosalind, *The Rāmāyaṇa of Vālmīki: An Epic of Ancient India*, vol. 4, *Kiṣkindhākāṇḍa*, Princeton: Princeton University Press, 1994.

Miller, Barbara D. and Alf Hiltebeitel (eds.), *Hair: Its Meaning and Power in Asian Cultures*, Albany: State University of New York Press, 1998.

Mudholkar, Shastri Shrinivas Katti (ed.), *Rāmāyaṇa of Vālmīki*, Bombay: Gujarati Printing Press, 1920.

Nath, Rai Bhadur Lala Baij, tr., *Adhyūtma-Rāmāyaṇa*, Allahabad: The Panini Office, 1913.

Panasikar, Wasudeva Laxman Sastri, *The Rāmāyana of Vālmīki*, 4th edn., Bombay: Nirṇayasāgar Press, 1930.

Pollock, Sheldon I, tr., *The Rāmāyaṇa of Vālmīki: An Epic of Ancient India*, vol. 2, *Ayodhyākāṇḍa*, ed. Robert P. Goldman, Princeton: Princeton University Press, 1986.

———, *Rāmāyana of Vālmīki: An Epic of Ancient India*, vol. 3, *Araṇyakāṇḍa*, ed. Robert P. Goldman, Princeton: Princeton University Press, 1991.

Raghunathan, N., tr., *Srimad Vālmīki Rāmāyaṇa*, vol. 2, Madras: Vighneswara Publishing House, 1981.

Ramanujan, A.K., 'Three Hundred Rāmāyanas', in *Many Rāmāyaṇas: The Diversity of a Narrative Tradition in South Asia*, Paula Richman (ed.), Berkeley: University of California Press, 1991. pp. 22-49.

Ṛgvedasaṁhitā, Pune: Vaidika Saṁśodhana Maṇḍala, 1933.

Roussel, Alfred, tr., *Le Rāmāyana de Vālmīki*, Paris: Librairie des cinq parties du monde, no. 7. 1903.

Shastri, Hari Prasad, tr., *The Rāmāyaṇa of Vālmīki*, 2nd edn., vol. 2, London: Shanti Sadan, 1969.

Simon, Richard, tr., *Die Erzählung vom grossen Affen Hanumat*, Saarbrücken: Universitätsbibliothek, 1977.

Śrīmad Vālmīki-Rāmāyana, Gorakhpur: Gita Press, 1969.

Śrīkṛṣṇadāsa, Gaṅgāviṣṇu (ed.), *Śrīmad Vālmīki-Rāmāyanaṁ*, Bombay: Lakṣmīveṅkaṭeśvara Mudraṇālaya, 1935.

Sundarakandam of Srimad Valmiki Ramayana, Madras: Sri Ramakrishna Math, 1983.

Sutherland, Sally J. (Goldman), 'The Bad Seed: Senior Wives and Elder Sons', in S.J. Sutherland (ed.), *Bridging Worlds: Studies on Women in South Asia*, Berkeley: Centres for South and Southeast Asia Studies (U. C. Berkeley), 1991, pp. 24-52.

Tapasyānanda, Swami, tr., *Sundarakandam of Srimad Valmiki Ramayana*, Madras: Sri Ramakrishna Math, 1983.

Varadacharya, K.S., *et al.* (eds.), *Śrīmad Vālmīki-Rāmāyanaṁ*, Mysore: University of Mysore, unpublished.

Vidyasagara, Pandit Jibananda (ed.), *Adhyātma-Rāmāyaṇa*, Calcutta: Valmiki Press, 1884.

List of Contributors

Robert Goldman is Professor of Sanskrit in the University of California at Berkeley. He is the author of *Gods, Priests, and Warriors: the Bhṛgus of the Mahābhārata* (New York: Columbia University Press, 1977), co-author of an introductory Sanskrit primer, *Devavāṇīpraveśikā: An Introduction to the Sanskrit Language* (Berkeley: Centre for South and Southeast Asia Studies, University of California at Berkeley, 1987), and has authored many scholarly articles on Sanskrit epic studies. A member of the American Academy of Arts and Sciences, he is perhaps most widely known as the General Editor and one of the principal translators of the ongoing collaborative translation of the *Vālmīki Rāmāyaṇa* (Princeton: Princeton University Press, 1985-), of which five of the projected seven volumes have thus far been published.

Alessandra Lopez y Royo did her Ph.D. in Art and Archaeology from the School of Oriental and African Studies, University of London. She has also studied the visual arts, archaeology and performance arts of both South and South-East Asia, has received practical training in a number of dance forms and has consistently published on all these topics over the past 10 years. She is at present Wingate Scholar at Wolfson College, University of Oxford where she is doing research on the iconography of Śiva images from Java and as Senior Researcher Officer at the University of Surrey-Roehampton she is contributing to a Leverhulme funded project on South Asian Dance in Britain. She has also recently researched a one year pilot project at the University of Surrey, Guildford, which investigated a computer animation of the dance reliefs of the ninth century CE. Prambanan complex, in Central Java. Her book, *Prambanan: Sculpture and Dance in Ancient Java* (Bangkok: White Lotus, 1998), is an introduction to this new research area, of equal value to art historians, archaeologists and performers.

Heidi Pauwels is Assistant Prof. in Hindi and Hinduism at the University of Washington in Seattle. Her interests include Hinduism and modern and medieval Hindi language and literature. A specialist in medieval *bhakti*, in particular Kṛṣṇa *bhakti* poetry in Braj, Dr. Pauwels has authored several articles on that topic and a full-length book, *Krishna's Round Dance Reconsidered: Harirām Vyās's Rāspañcādhyāyī* (London: Curzon, 1996). Close to completion is another book, *In Praise of Holy Men: Imagining Religious Communities in Medieval India,* which she plans to follow up with a study of Sitā.

Vidyut Aklujkar studied Sanskrit and Philosophy in the Universities of Poona, Tufts and British Columbia. She earned her Ph.D. in Philosophy in 1973. She is teaching in the department of Asian Studies and is a research associate at the Centre for India and South Asia Research at the University of British Columbia. Her research interest ranges from poetry to fiction to critical studies in Sanskrit and Marāṭhī literature. Also a poet, she has authored many scholarly articles, and her books include *The Primacy of Linguistic Units,* Indian Philosophical Quarterly No. 12. (Pune: Philosophy Dept., University of Poona, 1998), *Kāhānī,* a Marāṭhī novel (Pune: Deshmukh & Co. Publishers Private Ltd. 1998).

Sally J. Sutherland Goldman earned her Ph.D. from the University of California at Berkeley in 1979, where she is Lecturer in Sanskrit. She teaches Sanskrit at all levels as well as Buddhist Sanskrit, Pāli, and Prakrit at the University of California at Berkeley. She is the co-author of the *Devavāṇīpraveśikā: An Introduction to the Sanskrit Language.* She is Associate Editor of the *Vālmīki Rāmāyaṇa* Translation Project, annotator of the first book of the epic, the *Bālakāṇḍa,* and co-author of the fifth book, the *Sundarakāṇḍa* (Princeton: Princeton University Press, 1992-96). She is currently working on the sixth and seventh books of the epic. She is the editor of *Bridging Worlds: Studies on South Asian Women* (Berkeley: Center for South and Southeast Asia Studies, University of Berkeley at California, 1992), a collection of articles on the roles of women in South Asia and the co-editor of a new volume, *Themes in Indian History: The Sanskrit Epics* (Oxford University Press, forthcoming). Her area of interests are women studies, epic and classical Sanskrit literature, *vyākaraṇa* or Sanskrit grammar, and the Vedas. She has authored a number of articles in these areas.

Index

Fig. 1: View of Prambanan Complex

Fig. 2: Rāma wins Sītā's hand

Fig. 3: Dance at Bharata's coronation

Fig. 4: Sītā and one of her babies

Fig. 5: Rāma demonstrates skill to Sugrīva by shooting an arrow through seven trees, Hazāra Rāma Temple, Hampi

Fig. 6: Bālī & Sugrīva fighting, Hazāra Rāma Temple, Hampi

Fig. 7: Hazāra Rāma Temple, Vijaynagar

Fig. 8: Hazāra Rāma Temple, Vijaynagar

Fig. 9: Hazāra Rāma Temple, Vijaynagar

Fig. 10: Hazāra Rāma Temple, Vijaynagar